AND HALF THE SEED OF EUROPE

Mercer University Press

Endowed by

Tom Watson Brown

and

The Watson-Brown Foundation, Inc.

AND HALF THE SEED OF EUROPE

A Genealogy of the Great War, 1914–1918

Christopher Blake

Mercer University Press
Macon, Georgia
2017

MUP/ H945

Published by Mercer University Press
1501 Mercer University Drive
Macon, Georgia 31207

9 8 7 6 5 4 3 2 1

Books published by Mercer University Press are printed on acid-free paper that meets the requirements of the American National Standard for Information Sciences—Permanence of Paper for Printed Library Materials.

ISBN 978-0-88146-635-5
Cataloging-in-Publication Data is available from the Library of Congress

In Memory of the Soldiers of the Great War
And to Lewis Rae Blake and Samuel Holbrook Blake,
Two of their descendants

Contents

Acknowledgments

This book is the outcome of decades of personal interest in the First World War, as a consequence of my grandfathers' participation (a major theme of this book) and from my visiting the Western Front as an educator with several groups of school students. My former colleagues on those trips, Nick Cleaver and Andy Good, were central in helping me gain an understanding of the War, and those personal visits with them hold many fond memories.

In more recent years my father, Peter Blake, has been a primary inspiration for this book. To him I owe the gratitude that is due to a loving father, and also to a wise teacher of family lives and living. His direct connection to my grandfathers' generation and his detailed knowledge of them have motivated me to tell their story, and hopefully through it the telling of a broader story of a forgotten generation and its significance. And Carolyn, my sister, has been extremely helpful in sending information and memorabilia from the U.K. to support my writing.

Deep gratitude is also extended to Koenraad (Conrad) Dumoulin, a professional guide to the battlefields of Flanders. Not only was Conrad's knowledge and passion inspirational, but also his willingness to guide a return visit to Walter Gower's grave in 2015 provided new historical information. That visit fundamentally shifted my understanding and that of my family for nearly a century, of the circumstances of his service and sacrifice in the War.

More recently, my friends and colleagues in Georgia have listened patiently to my ideas, read some of my writings, offered feedback and given encouragement. In particular, Kirby Godsey, Hank Huckaby, Larry Walker and Neil Cullinan have expressed the conviction that there is much value to the concept behind this book, and their confidence has helped focus my thinking. For clarifying important military details, I am indebted to two individuals at Fort Benning, Georgia: Dave Stieghan, U.S. Army Infantry Branch Historian, and Colonel Bill Carty, Deputy Commandant. My assistant, Carey Wimberly, has managed my priorities and my calendar with patience and skill, ensuring that the book trail never went cold; my colleague, Frances Marine Davis, has been generous in offering documentary advice; and my intern, Mary Awoyeye, has been an excellent clerical assistant in the drafting.

And Melody has believed in this book from the moments of its genesis, and unwaveringly supported me on its journey. She has my loving thanks.

All of these people and groups can take some credit for this book reaching publication, and others too whom I cannot identify by name. For the book's doubtless shortcomings in scholarship and syntax, however, they are exempted. For those I am responsible as its author.

THE PARABLE OF THE OLD MAN AND THE YOUNG

So Abram rose, and clave the wood, and went,
And took the fire with him, and a knife.
And as they sojourned both of them together,
Isaac the first-born spake and said, My Father,
Behold the preparations, fire and iron,
But where the lamb for this burnt-offering?
Then Abram bound the youth with belts and
    strops,
And builded parapets and trenches there,
And stretched forth the knife to slay his son.
When lo! an angel called him out of heaven,
Saying, Lay not thy hand upon the lad,
Neither do anything to him. Behold,
A ram, caught in a thicket by its horns;
Offer the Ram of Pride instead of him.
But the old man would not so, but slew his son,
And half the seed of Europe, one by one.

Wilfred Owen
1918

GUNNER LEWIS BLAKE'S WORKING ROUTINE

8-inch howitzers of the 39th Siege Battery, Royal Garrison Artillery conducting a shoot in the Fricourt-Mametz Valley, August 1916, during the Battle of the Somme

---

LEWIS BLAKE, GRANDFATHER POPS

A characteristic smiling pose of my grandfather, veteran gunner of the British artillery of the Great War, in his later years, ebullient and full of vigor.

Family photo, likely taken at a family celebration in the 1980's, by one of my relatives. Now the possession of my father, Peter Blake.

HORACE THE FAMILY MAN

My grandfather with his young children, my mother Patricia (Paddy) and my uncle Ken.

Family photo, likely taken by my grandmother Mabel Wood (Drywood).

THE WAR TO END ALL WARS?

Joseph Ambrose, an 86-year-old World War I veteran, attends the dedication day parade for the Vietnam Veterans Memorial in 1982. He is holding the flag that covered the casket of his son, who was killed in the Korean War. November 13, 1982.

Department of Defense. Defense Audiovisual Agency; Scene Camera Operator: Mickey Sanborn.

WHERE THE POPPIES BLOW

"Blood Swept Lands and Seas of Red" was an installation by ceramic artist Paul Cummins, with setting by stage designer Tom Piper. It was officially unveiled on 5 August 2014, one hundred years since the first full day of Britain's involvement in the First World War, and by 11 November would have 888,246 ceramic poppies in the moat around the Tower of London, each poppy representing a British or Colonial military fatality during the war.

SHADOWS ACROSS THE GENERATIONS

My father, Peter, visits the grave of Private Walter Gower, his Great Uncle, on the centennial of his death in late April 2015 at Bailleul Communal Cemetery, Nord, in France.

Personal photograph of the author

Preface

One of life's mysteries is that we people experience it both uniquely and collectively. For example, if we consider the desperate refugee crisis arising from the Syrian civil war, it is obvious that our human family is collectively impacted, yet that impact is uniquely different for each of us. Sitting in my comfortable office in Macon on a Monday morning, the impact on me is solely in terms of intellectual pondering, emotional disturbance and professional confusion on how to implement official policy restrictions on international students coming to my public university. For a refugee family stranded in a make-shift camp in Turkey, or worse still stranded in Aleppo, the impact is truly terrifying and tragic.

Different disciplines have navigated this binary nature of human experience over the centuries. For example, literary characters still speak to us across the centuries in powerful existential ways, and yet without having existed physically as actual events or persons bound by time and place. Our subjective insights into common human emotions and experiences are a wealth of opportunity for the literary novelist and play-write, and we connect them in our own ways to the world as we—both individually and collectively—know it. Shakespeare translates across the centuries for this same reason.

Empirical disciplines have of course sought to describe that same world in different terms. Whether in the search for irrefutable laws of the universe, or a unified theory of physics, or geological explorations of our environment or the establishment of constitutional government that stands the test of time, the human quest has still sought an understanding of reality as it actually presents itself, both human and physical. Here the objective nature of life challenges us in myriad ways to make sense of our own lives against a grander backdrop, a cosmic canvas that will outlast us, a human history that stretches across eons and in which, as Walt Whitman noted, "...the powerful play goes on, and you may contribute a verse ."

I am not a professional historian, and am very hesitant to claim how historians view this continuum between human objectivity and subjectivity, and make sense of earlier human lives both singularly and globally. I know that history in a sense values our human past, and this book can be seen as part of that same valuing. But I am sure that whatever criteria history embraces for itself are likely absent to some degree here. This book thus does not claim the identity of historical scholarship, but rather provides a reflective, interpretative stance on personal history in the context of a shared human past. It also posits that in looking at our past—globally and singularly—we can discern a more potent understanding of how we have been shaped as agents of our lives both collectively and individually by the choices of our forebears.

As a child I do not think I learned that way about the past. I did take many classes in history at school, and learned about fascinating events that appeared on the "canvas" so to speak. They were pivotal events that swept across the arc of time and changed that arc as it moved onwards. I liked this approach very much, and in it I learned and appreciated much that western education reports about human life in the earlier centuries, particularly in the western hemisphere. Persons with names such as Martin Luther, Napoleon, and Churchill were studied, but I learned about them not as individuals but rather in terms of the consequences of their lives in shaping events of large-scale importance. And so, Churchill became learned as a global figure rather than a fascinating mosaic of a man. Truth told, individuals were viewed in terms of power and change, and so many others were ignored in this grand tapestry view of our human past. In this way I learned about the First World War, as a global war of catastrophic consequence, a time when the "old" gave way to the "new," and as a painful event that old men, including our grandfathers, knew at first hand.

The discipline and methodology of history has doubtless changed since my youth but that is not my purpose here. What interests me is the experience of less known individuals within that grand tapestry, and how their lives affected the future, both intimately and as part of a larger picture. In particular, the persons that I met or learned about as members of families, those grandfathers and their loved ones who knew directly the global trauma of the First World War, provide the context and conduit for understanding that War and its importance. Why families? It strikes me that talking about our families—or genealogy to be precise—empowers us in ways that are often overlooked, and I mean empower both individually and collectively as nations, peoples and groups. World religions understand this. The Abrahamic faiths of Judaism, Christianity and Islam are rooted in powerful genealogical stories of belief and experience. So are Buddhism and Hinduism, grounded in the family events of Prince Siddhartha or Lord Krishna respectively. These families provided the founding and inspiration of faiths for millennia across the world, as well as for art, poetry and music.

Genealogy then is the lens through which I revisit in this book an extraordinary cataclysm in human history, the "Great War," a name that began to take form even while the conflict was still engaged. What then does genealogy offer to us in viewing such a global event from the distance of one century? Several tools become available.

Firstly, it gives us the means of recognizing that our lives are balanced between both structure and agency, as the social scientists might put it. We are agents of choice, but our structure is given to us. Oftentimes, the courageous choices that inspire or catalyze entire social movements—such as Rosa Parks' refusal to abide by segregationist mandates in Montgomery, Alabama—are rooted not only in the cause they advance, but in the reality of an individual having had enough of injustice on a personal level. That same reality occurred in the War, where the great choices of the past came to a titanic consequence. We see ourselves as free, but we are also part of a human chain, in which certain givens exist. That means that our stories are both unique, but also generalizable. We can find in our families the seeds of our own life literally, but also the roots of our thinking and behaving. That occurs singularly and globally. Indeed, the Great War could have proceeded by different routes, but it was borne out of structure and previous decision-making, and not simply a random event. The Archduke's assassination on 28 June 1914 may have been a small and partially random event but its occurrence was a detail of a broader, connected narrative of action and consequence over many decades.

Secondly, genealogy is democratic. It provides a stage for any individual who lived during the Great War to stand alongside Kaiser, King, or Czar, and thus understands that history is about real people, not simply a collective or famous event. In this book there are several vignettes offered about individuals. Those vignettes are not intended simply to be romanticized or quaint descriptions of loved ones. Instead they are meant to show how people lived their lives in the shadow of the War. Moreover, how they lived their lives differently, as a result of that War.

Thirdly, genealogy gives us a mirror on ourselves. It shows us that we may have a line in the play, but the play is bigger than our words and actions and that we are shaped very much by the lines leading up to our moment on the stage. Psychotherapy might have suggested for the past hundred years that our parents were all important to our life habits, but genealogy has surely described the importance of our roots for much longer and in more enriched ways.

And finally, genealogy motivates and inspires. We are, in the end, people who cherish intimacy and love. We exist in relationship to others. Even a War leader such as Sir John French, as we see later, treasured the love of his sister and made sense of his life both in terms of grand battles and private family. In this sense, the trauma of the War has been felt across the ages and through the generations. It has shaped the world not only in the halls of governments, but around family kitchen tables. It spurred on new ways of acting not only in national policies, but in parental decisions. Genealogy allows us to see how this happened. Even in the smallness of our everyday events lie the clues to our past, present and future, and how the human family will be changed by the short line we each utter in the larger play of our world's landscape.

The Great War is one hundred years old. It is distant enough to be forgotten to our minds, and near enough to be living in our souls. It is time that our minds and our souls were united in understanding how and who we are today as a result of an event, a Great War, that changed history and millions of families forever.

1.

DOUGHBOY HEROES ON COLEMAN HILL

Macon, Georgia, resides in the very middle of the state, a few miles above the "Gnat Line." This ecological boundary is the vestige of an ancient and long relocated coastline, south of which is infested with gnats during the summer months, north of which is thankfully clear. Equally ancient, the Ocmulgee River slowly drains southward through Macon and for thousands of years gave sustenance to the local Native American Creek and Mississippian tribes. Their settlement on the banks of the Ocmulgee left us with the finest and largest Indian Mounds in the nation, at the Ocmulgee National Historic Park. More recently, Macon endured Sherman's March to the Sea on route from Atlanta to Savannah during the Civil War, but fortunately was spared its devastation. Macon-Bibb County has a population of about 100,000 and is the home of Southern music—the Song and Soul of the South is its tag line. The melodies and rhythms of Otis Brown, Little Richard, and the Allman Brothers among others originate in Macon. From my professional vantage point, it is also the home of some great institutions of higher learning: the newest public university in the state, Middle Georgia State University, where I work as its president; Mercer University, the home of the Bears and some outstanding musicians, lawyers and medics; Wesleyan College, the world's oldest women's college and sometime alma mater of Madame Chiang Kai-shek; and Central Georgia Technical College, one of the most entrepreneurial technical colleges in the region. A few miles south in neighboring Houston County sits the large and vital Robins Air Force Base. Macon is the home of a strong and thriving community, with a long and mixed past and a bright future.

Above downtown is one of the highest hills for many miles, likely carved as a bluff of the Ocmulgee River. Its overlook provides a stellar vista of downtown Macon, and is the location of Coleman Hill Park, where on Sundays in the sweltering summer people listen to rock concerts and children can zoom down the curving slide built into the hill. Behind Coleman Hill, with the most resplendent view of all, is the antebellum Cowles-Woodruff House on the National Historic Register, used by General Wilson as his headquarters during the Civil War occupation. Next to the Cowles-Woodruff home is the Furman Smith Law Library of Mercer University, whose cupola is a landmark for miles and signals a beacon of Southern gentility and academic pride.

In the winter of 2014 I found myself exploring Coleman Hill Park. I had moved to Macon at a difficult time of personal and professional transition, grateful for a new opportunity and chapter in life as the head of a very promising regional university. But, in truth, week-ends had too many hours of empty time and to fill those I often engaged in many solitary walks of exploration around my new home. Halfway down the hill I found two memorials, one dedicated to the longest serving Georgia politician in the U.S. House of Representatives, Carl Vinson. The other memorial immediately struck me with surprise and intrigue. With marble elegance and austere chamber-like design, it was a powerful construction dedicated to the 151st Machine Gun Battalion of the Rainbow Division. On a brass plaque at the top of the memorial were listed the seventy-three names of the fallen of the War 1917–1918, the years of United States engagement in the First World War. Around the very top of the memorial are engraved in the marble the nine major engagements of combat of the 151st battalion in northern Europe: Luneville; Baccarat; Esperance; Champagne; Aisne-Marne; Saint Mihiel; Esseypannes; Argonne; and Army of Occupation. The memorial appeared unkempt. Its flower beds were full of weeds, and the sod had over the years grown to cover over the engraved dedication at its base.

The memorial's existence should not be underestimated. There are scant few memorials or statues to the memory of the fallen of the first global conflict in the USA. Some states have none. An internet search typically yields a figure of around fifty memorials. Only in late 2014, 100 years after the conflict had erupted in Europe, did President Barack Obama authorize the creation of a national World War I memorial in Washington, D.C. to commemorate the 120,000 dead Americans of that War, and remind us too of the third of a million other casualties.

Public memorials enjoy a much larger presence, reputation and role in European cultures. The Cenotaph in Whitehall, the Menin Gate war memorial at Ypres, the awe-strikingly enormous Monument to the Missing of the Somme, the Canadian memorial on Vimy Ridge: these and other international treasures have literally shaped our thinking and seeing of the War from the pained side of history. I have on several occasions visited Tyne Cot Cemetery and Memorial to the Missing, now complete with a museum, which is located directly on the Passchendaele battlefield of the Ypres salient. It is the largest cemetery in the world for British Commonwealth forces of any war, containing the graves of 12,000 dead, 8,400 of which are unnamed or "known unto God," as the epitaph reads. In short, the British, the French, and, to a lesser extent, the Germans realized that the Great War needed great memorializing, and the countries of Europe contain magnificent and somber statements in stone to that process. The United States, for good reason, did not begin this process so extensively after 1919. It was therefore noteworthy that an exception to this was once clearly intended on Coleman Hill in a permanent memorial beautifully placed high above Macon, in honor of the local Doughboys who joined their Allies in France in the last quarter of the conflict.

On that cold January afternoon it was clear that Macon's legacy of remembering its war dead was once special, and yet was full of poignancy, especially since its rare monument seemed neglected and forgotten: rather like the War itself on this side of the Atlantic. I start this story there at the Coleman Hill memorial, not because it has personal history, but because rather than a closed memorial it became the gateway to larger memories, grounded in family and personal experience. For "The War to End All Wars" and its current centennial commemoration is intimate as well as a global event that reaches our lives, individually and collectively, across the decades that have led us to this day. The phrase "Their Name Liveth for Evermore" is from the deuterocanonical book of Ecclesiasticus.[1] It ends a verse that reads with hope, "Their bodies are buried in peace; but their name liveth for evermore." The British writer Rudyard Kipling, after the Great War in which he lost his son, recommended this phrase as the national memorial emblem for Britain and its Empire, to begin a process of healing and making sense of the conflict. The famous architect Edward Lutyens was thus inspired to create fitting stone expressions that in engraved rock asserted time and time again, "Their Name Liveth for Evermore." Maybe those seventy-three names of Macon's fallen on Coleman Hill can also be honored in spirit with that epitaph.

This book is thus an attempt to co-join memory and meaning. More informed historical analysis can be found elsewhere surrounding the 1914–1918 War, and

---

[1] "Their bodies are buried in peace; but their name liveth for evermore," Ecclesiasticus (Sirach) 44:14.

the centennial of the war continues to bring new scholarly insights into the War. Instead, this book is a memoir and genealogy, and how that genealogy was shaped by, and gives interpretation to the significance of, one of the greatest calamities of human history. The direct memory of the War as a participating combatant died in the first decade of this century. With the passing of the last veteran from all combatant nations in 2010, surprisingly a woman, the Great War forever passed from being living human memory to that of recounted history. But genealogy, which gives each generation the chance to engage with the lives of our preceding generations, remains a doorway into understanding the impacted lives of those who helped create us. Moreover, in understanding the lives of those in our genealogy, and their hopes and fears, we also understand ourselves better. Thankfully, none of us experienced World War I, and many did not experience subsequent conflicts either. But the point is that our mothers, grandmothers, fathers, and grandfathers did. Because they did, they were different, and so are we. One hundred years later it is timely to consider how the Great War still reaches us individually and collectively today, from beyond the graves of those whose lives were tossed violently and prematurely asunder, and now also from beyond the graves of those who returned and grew weary through age. Their story is part of ours too. It is one that teaches us that the past is at the heart of our present, and that our present will indeed be handed on, for better or worse, to our children and their children. A city set on a hill cannot be hid, scripture cites. The monument of Coleman Hill is strikingly visible to all. It is an apt time to revisit its presence and significance.

AWAITING ORDERS: THE FIRST DAY OF THE BATTLE OF THE SOMME

A ration party of the Royal Irish Rifles in a communication trench during the Battle of the Somme. The date is believed to be 1 July 1916, the first day of the infamous Battle of the Somme, and the unit is possibly the 1st Battalion, Royal Irish Rifles (25th Brigade, 8th Division) awaiting movement to forward trenches on 1 July, 1916

Imperial War Museum, UK Government, Photo Q1 (Collection 1900-02)

2.

Age Shall Not Weary Them, Nor The Years Condemn

An enduring paradox is that as we age we realize the generations that preceded us are more close and familiar to us than they seemed when we were young. We age, and in aging we understand incrementally and better who they were before us, and who we are. Youth makes us feel worth a freshly-minted billion dollars, but we grow smart and valuable through the tarnishing of that glossy allure. Like many, I was blessed with being born into a stable multi-generational, middle class family in London. Born in 1960 meant I was too young to recall the upheaval of that decade, but enjoyed all the norms of the era of post-war affluence and the later era of pre-digital confusion. The middle of the 20th century was a time to thank Providence that two world wars were done and won, that our Western alliances were strong in the face of Soviet tyranny and that the future held promise.

My family was fortunate to reflect this optimistic outlook. Born into a family of four children, and being the third, I was thankfully molded by usual healthy experiences of parents who enjoyed love and life, and good relationships with healthy siblings and nearby grandparents. When I was two-years old my maternal grandfather passed away, his passing linked to lung damage sustained in World War I. But the dominant image of grandparents remained static and reassuring in my early years. I loved both grandmothers, but it was my two grandfathers who provided a defining set of recollections and inspirations for this genealogy.

My maternal father, Horace Holbrook Wood, died relatively early in his mid-60s, and I have only one clear memory of him. I recall a tartan blanket, and me lying on it looking up at him. It must have been when I was two, because he died in late 1962, when his lungs finally expired nearly a half century after incurring injuries from mustard gas on the Western Front. Stories in my family abound of a great, humane, well-read man of professional success, who managed to sustain his refrigeration business and his employees' livelihoods during the Great Depression. There is an enduring family image of him in a black and white photo, in middle age with receding hair, and like many of his generation smoking his pipe while smiling at something out of camera view. In the War he was enlisted in the mounted (horseback) infantry, an anachronistic form of warfare in an age of machine gun, flamethrower, and massive shelling. But horse warfare was the means that Field Marshall Douglas "Butcher" Haig insisted was the key to victory, even if it originated from military strategy of preceding centuries and could be deemed partly responsible for the two million deaths in those battles where the logic of Haig prevailed. Whatever history's split opinion of Haig, he is a figure that the American General John J. Pershing said was responsible "for winning the war," and my grandfather Horace Wood was part of Haig's strategy for that victory, even with a horse.

Horace Holbrook survived all four years of the war. But history has a way of changing the view of the past, and his survival took a toll on his future. In today's vernacular, he is a figure we might have conjectured suffered from Post-Traumatic Stress Disorder to some extent. Family stories abound of him enduring terrifying and exhausting nightmares with some frequency for the rest of his life. The nature of his nightmares was not known. But one clue resides in a small gold medallion I have in my possession. It belonged, according to family story, to his very best friend in the mounted infantry. During one attack, with my grandfather and his friend still in their saddles, an enemy shell landed nearby. Horace was unscathed, but his nameless friend was instantly killed through decapitation from the shell-burst. One can only imagine the trauma of choosing to remove a symbol of affection from the shredded, gore-ridden corpse, but his love and honor for his comrade appears to have been sufficient motivation. His friend, whose name is unknown, was a Roman Catholic, and Horace kept his friend's gold medallion of the Virgin Mary as a sacred memento of their friendship. I have inherited that medallion and keep it cherished in my home. Since he died in 1962 he probably does not count in the statistics of the War casualties, but the use of terror in the form of mustard gas produced its wicked results in his death from lung disease 44 years later in suburban London. He was politically centrist, extremely well-read, loved discussions on politics and life, and was a man of good books, great conversations and virtuous generosity. He was by all accounts a much-loved man and a faithful Christian, and my second son Samuel Holbrook Blake was given his name partly in his honor.

My memory and relationship with my paternal grandfather, my paternal, was much stronger. Lewis (Lew) Blake shared some common biographical facts with Horace Wood. Both born in 1898, they each enlisted prematurely believing like many that a short war would be a noble and exhilarating way of proving youthful patriotic duty. Similarly, they each served virtually the full duration of the war (1914–18), and returned home externally unscathed and able to re-build lives as successful productive citizens, spouses and fathers. Even though the British casualties by Christmas 1914 had already exceeded the entire size of the pre-existing 250,000-strong standing, professional British army—the "Old Contemptibles" as the Prussian Generals mocked them—both young men were predictably swept along with the euphoria of jingoism and public clamor. My paternal grandfather Lewis Blake was sent to Salisbury Plain military camp for eight weeks of training in the cold autumn rain of Wiltshire, England, and was assigned to the artillery, first as Bombardier Gunner and eventually Corporal Blake. Later in his life he would use the phrase "Salisbury Plain weather" to describe those biting days of rain, wind, and persistent winter-like temperatures. He was shipped to France on 2 January 1915 and then fired and took incoming artillery fire on his seventeenth birthday that same month. He became a communications runner, moving between the front line trenches and artillery positions, a role that facilitated not only exchange of information but also trading of goods, which I revisit later. He kept the same horse for four years, named it Satan because it was a "devil of an animal to train," and was ordered by his superiors to shoot it when embarking for Britain after the hostilities ceased in late 1918. I do not know if he shot his "Satan," but I do know that he talked very little of the Great War for the rest of his long life of ninety-two years. What I have recounted here is almost the summation of spoken exchanges on War information, except for a few stories about hunting eggs and sunken "petit bateaux" (small boats). His was a good and productive life like Horace's, incorporating both professional and family success and the tragedy of losing two children to accidents. He would rarely reflect on the meaning or experience of the War, except telling me just once that "nothing in life could begin to come close to the nature of those experiences"; then he was silent until the grave. When he chose to drink wine, it was always sweet Sauternes, preferably Barsac, which he discovered as a young Tommy (the English generic name of a soldier) over in France. I loved my "Pops," his verbal charm, his unstoppable will, his restless activity, and his bullish manner. My eldest son, Lewis Rae Blake, took his name partly in his honor.

A third immediate member of my family genealogy was not so fortunate in the bare outline of his War experience. This family member never returned from the killing fields of Belgium and France, and yet his cut-short life and story is as important in our family history as anyone else's. Indeed, his impact decades later on my family narrative was perhaps the greatest in terms of finding a family meaning in the Great War. This individual was my Great, Great Uncle, Walter Gower, from the county of Kent, often referred to as the Garden of England and the county nearest continental Europe. Walter was the young and much-loved uncle of my maternal grandmother, Mabel. Family births over the years had arranged that Uncle Walter was merely eight years older than my grandmother and as a young girl she adored her Uncle. In 1914 my fifteen year-old grandmother watched twenty-two year old Walter join the hundreds of thousands of eager volunteers for France, and his keenness to serve was rewarded with an assignment as a Private soldier in the 2nd infantry battalion of the famous East Kent Regiment, more popularly known as the Buffs for their leather belts, enjoying 400 years of regimental history dating to 1571 and the Reformation struggles for the soul of western Christianity in continental Holland.

My grandmother, known to us as Nana, was by all accounts heartbroken that her beloved Uncle Walter never returned from Flanders. Shortly after the War she began a long and happy marriage with Horace Holbrook, the mounted infantry veteran and casualty of mustard gas. On learning of his new bride's grief over her lost Uncle, Horace returned to Flanders alone in the early 1920s to locate successfully Walter's grave in honor of his new wife, Mabel, the site at that time marked with a wooden cross. During my childhood I would occasionally hear my grandmother reference the life and loss of Private Walter Gower, and disappointingly learn that his gravesite was now lost to family memory. There was no record of his burial location and no knowledge of the circumstances of the ultimate sacrifice he made.

For some eighty-five years the grave of Walter Gower remained unknown and unvisited by my family, but in 1995 I learned that Britain's Commonwealth War Graves Commission had achieved the extraordinary feat of publishing an online database of all dead of Britain, its Empire and later Commonwealth from its 20th and 21st Century wars. Within ten minutes of logging onto the search engine of the CWGC the decades of uncertainty were replaced by unambiguous and immediate information on Walter's burial location. His resting place was a communal cemetery in Bailleul, France, near to a sanatorium that had acted as a major field hospital of the Ypres salient. His death at the age of twenty-three occurred on 25 April 1915, and his full regimental details were clearly recorded. Two immediate actions resulted from this new information after the years of uncertainty. First was a call to my parents, with a promise that I would coordinate an early visit to his grave. Second was a harder task, namely to identify the historical circumstances of his military death. A pilgrimage to his resting place would be more meaningful if we knew how he had paid the ultimate sacrifice, and whether his tiny experience and demise could be cast into the broader context of the more universal and historical human act that was the Great War of 1914–1918. In a larger sense, though, the discovery in the late 1990s of Walter's resting place provided a focal point of renewed interest and story-telling. Years of ignorance, momentarily removed, awakened a renewed sense of our family, its history, its stories, and its pains. A new genealogy was possible.

The conversations, experiences and information that can be gleaned from these three men, whose DNA is part of mine, and whose experiences were common to millions of a bygone age, can tell us something of life, family, and meaning of how those were affected by the 1914–1918 War. They are not the only characters I shall highlight. Indeed, my own relationship over thirty years with the fields of Flanders has shaped largely my own understanding of the Great War. There are two ways that I believe this genealogy works in informing my thoughts. Firstly, the stories of the originators themselves are its foundation. Lewis, Horace, and Walter had first-hand experience of a conflict that has now passed forever from memory to history, but their foundational experiences of that War remain the primary source for its interpretation. But there is also a secondary source at work here that gives power to genealogy, namely that events of the past shape other persons, are re-told through the prism of those others' lives, cause ripples across the lives and decades of families and communities, and thus take on an additional significance. Such is the case in my own life, where I have visited the battlefields as both guide and visitor, and now in the United States have also been fortunate to hear the genealogies of Americans whose fathers and grandfathers were protagonists of that War. In short, the Great War stands within the identities and lives of our participating ancestors, but it also brings us a century later into an encounter with it, and a search to explain its meaning, in our intimacy with families and friends through the mystery of time. In their – and our –stories are fragments and windows into a universal, global story, narrated and shone as through a prism to us personally through family genealogy. What that story tells us of the human experience—then and now—and its origins in a supremely pivotal and painful event in the history of the human species is the stuff of what follows.

THE YPRES SALIENT AT THE OUTSET OF THE BATTLE OF PASSCHENDAELE (THIRD YPRES) IN LATE SUMMER 1917

Two British pack mules carrying shells struggle through the mud in the Ypres salient on the Western Front, August, 1917 at the early stages of the Battle of Passchendaele. The battle was to become forever associated with atrocious conditions of rain and mud, and extraordinary numbers of casualties on both sides.

Imperial War Museum, UK Government, Photo Q 5941

3.

Garden Lawns and Flanders Fields

Lewis Blake (Pops) died at the age of 92 in 1990 and he rests in a cemetery in Wellingborough, England. His life had spanned more than ninety percent of the extraordinary twentieth-century, having been born on 24 January 1898 in Sandy, England, some fifty miles north of London in rural Bedfordshire. I had known him intimately as a grandfather for thirty years, and had lived within an hour's drive of him throughout that time. Our parents' expectations of children's responsibilities toward their grandparents were usual: weekly or fortnightly visits, holiday meals together, birthday cards, presents, etc. One particular expectation involved visits to Pops' house in suburban London. Like many houses built in the 1920s, this one was a dignified single home, with a front and rear garden (yard) and established trees. These visits were sometimes tedious for a child. Patience, manners and attentiveness were expected, probably as a hangover from the Victorian "seen-but-not-heard" attitude toward children. Today's child-centered bias and perhaps angst seems light years distant. One overriding memory is being expected to visit Pops' greenhouse, providing a break to sitting at the kitchen table.

Lewis Blake was very fond of his greenhouse. Britain's temperate climate has always encouraged horticulture, and mid-century England was a crowded island where allotments, gardens, and lawns provided outside recreation. Environment and tender care could indeed produce aesthetics in the garden, and Pops was skilled in that endeavor. His greenhouse was large, and sub-sectioned. Although the English climate varies considerably less than continental North America, a greenhouse afforded protection from winter frosts, and conversely summer Mediterranean-like warmth with daytime highs, with an extended growing season. In the yard itself, my grandfather took pride in a quintessential English lawn, beds of flowers and shrubs that were indicative of higher skill and greater care than many others showed. The lawn itself was of such high quality, and cared for diligently with the aid of an elderly gardener, that it was pristine enough for the game of bowls. Bowls is an established English recreational sport of genteel elegance. Today's Olympic sport of curling gives a similar notion, but with more energy and executed on ice instead of grass. Memories of English summers include images of men and women in white jackets rolling large brown bowls on a village green toward a smaller ivory-colored jack ball, with the purpose of landing closest to the jack. My grandfather had a set of bowls, and his immaculate lawn was perfect for the game, adding welcome excitement to our visits. At the end of his lawn was a trellis-framed entrance to an intriguing area. Behind tall shrubs he stored his lawn equipment and other ancillary yard debris. Behind that space, with even more appeal and mystery, ran a stream with hedges around it that provided the border to his property, with other slightly visible homes secluded behind the other bank. This area was the most appealing and ominous in the yard. The stream wandered to an unknown destination, and its banks were muddy, shrouded in roots and weeds. The water depth was unknown, and on particularly risky days my brothers and I would grab a pair of rubber "wellies" (boots) so we could risk wading in the stream.

Ventures to the stream were full of adrenaline rushes. In going there we pushed into a nether region with a water boundary, and then returned to the light and safety of the garden, with abundant questions about the stream and its destination. The greenhouse has one overriding memory, of the color of red. Specifically, the long seasons of bloom that the greenhouse provided for Pops' favorite plant, the Geranium, or Pelargonium. The British tend to have a love-affair with the Geranium, with some justification since they respond dramatically well to the Gulf Stream tempered climate of the British Isles, except for winter when a few weeks of frost will kill them unless protected within the harbor of a greenhouse. Geraniums provide stunning color of many varieties and mixtures. They delightfully stretch our incredulity that nature can provide such vibrant, exploding color. My grandfather Pops appreciated this quality, too, since my striking memory is a greenhouse full of red Geraniums. Occasionally he would half-heartedly grow the odd white or pink variety, but his greenhouse was a year-round tendered pasture of red bloom.

His house had one other interesting feature, an attic that had a hidden door entrance. Inside it was dark and full of relics of his life. We were discouraged by our father not to venture there. That of course enhanced its mystique like that of the muddy stream. This was another place of ominous portent and strange items. As children we always would look for an excuse and moment to wander upstairs. The stream and the attic were the rewards of curiosity during childhood visits that were otherwise dutiful and dull. I visited his house numerous times in my childhood, until Pops moved in his early 80s to a smaller bungalow (ranch home) near to his oldest son and daughter-in-law, my uncle Ed and aunt Mary. During those childhood visits, which dwindled in frequency during adolescence, I formed a picture of a cheerful grandfather, with a fascinating yard and house, and who talked incessantly on topics and events that I did not know. But those stories were mainly of his past, decades earlier, when his geraniums were not growing, when his pipe and tobacco were not at hand, and when he had youth in his limbs. That youth had existed some six decades earlier, and his house gave clues to his past.

Lewis Blake had entered the Great War like many millions of young men around Europe, believing in its inherent rightness and its inevitable short success. Like my other grandfather, Horace, he had lied about his age in order to be admitted to the fighting cause. British regulations formally prevented military enlistment until seventeen years, and combat operations only after the age of eighteen. In late August 1914 he entered the recruitment office to enlist. When asked his age, he informed the sergeant at the table that he would be seventeen in January, to which the recruitment sergeant told him to leave, walk around the block, and return in a few minutes with a different age. So Lewis Blake on second attempt was admitted that day to the British army as a volunteer, and sent off days later to basic training on Salisbury Plain, a major British army camp still operational today and close to the famous and ancient Celtic Stonehenge. His "Salisbury Plain weather" references for the rest of his days were built on the twelve weeks of sodden and punishing training he undertook there.

He embarked on Boxing Day—26 December—for Dover, with thousands of other British, Empire and Irish volunteers, and days later was headed for a battlefront that was developing into a different and ominous formation. By Christmas of 1914, Britain and its Empire countries had been at war with Germany and Austria-Hungary for four months, a timeframe most had voiced sufficient to teach the German Kaiser a lesson and conclude an Allied victory. Germany's reliance on the generation-old Schlieffen Plan as the basic structure to its War strategy had required German interference in neutral Belgium. The Balkan crisis of July after the 28 June assassination of Archduke Franz Ferdinand and his wife Sophie, the heir to the Habsburg dynasty of Austria-

Hungary, had already embroiled the major World Powers in a lock-step, domino-style sleepwalk to war and triggered a machine-like continental war march. The causes and catalysts of the Great War have long been the subject of historical scholarship. What is not debatable is that the powers of Europe were primed militarily for conflict long before its commencement, and that the conditions were ripe for a tinder box incendiary to its start. That tinder box was Franz Ferdinand's assassination, ironically he being the most dovish of Austro-Hungarian leaders. The ensuing determination of Austria-Hungary to punish small Serbia for its assumed and unproven official role in the assassination was the domino that fell as a result of the assassination. Since Germany was committed to Austria-Hungary, and Russia to Serbia, it was obvious that a small proxy war had bigger and more dangerous ramifications. Five weeks after the assassination, Germany's ruthless application of the Schlieffen Plan to attack France by circumventing its fortifications via neutral Belgium meant that Britain's 1839 promise to protect Belgium was the trigger for a wider European War. As Sir Edward Grey, Foreign Secretary for Great Britain put it on 3 August 1914, "The lamps are going out all over Europe: we shall not see them lit again in our lifetime." The awful, irony is that three direct grandsons of Great Britain's Queen Victoria were each monarchs in charge of three major combatants: Kaiser Wilhelm II of Germany; Tsar Nicholas of Russia; and George V of Great Britain. Their enfeebled telegrams during the crisis and promises to seek a peaceful resolution did nothing to prevent mobilization on all fronts, and in the heady logic of war theory one hundred years ago, mobilization was akin to pushing a large snowball down an avalanche-ready Alpine mountain. The momentum, direction, and destination were obvious.

Lewis Blake was a young man during these days of the July crisis that Winston Churchill, at that time the First Lord of Admiralty, described as "the most dramatic month the world had known." Lewis' transition from voluntary recruitment to Salisbury boot camp to the Flanders fields would have followed a seamless logistical path. It would have also reminded him powerfully of the weather and war conditions that were to prevail not only on Salisbury Plain but across the English Channel in Flanders. That region of northern Europe became eponymous with tragedy on epic proportions, and like the War itself, ignored national boundaries to include Belgium, France and disputed regions stretching back centuries. The route to Flanders was quick, involving train and ship across the Channel as part of the British Expeditionary Force. The proximity was particularly striking for troops on leave returning from the front, since they could be in the trenches killing the enemy in the morning, and at the London Ritz or Fortnum & Mason cafeteria for dinner in the evening.

One can only surmise what sixteen-year old Lewis Blake was thinking and feeling by New Year of 1915, since no written or oral record survived, but the realities of the War were surely stark enough to impact even such a young mind. By Christmas, the casualty rate on what was to become famed as the Western Front, originally a German title, was bewildering. Prior to the War the standing British army, one of the best prepared and equipped, numbered less than one third of a million men, tiny in comparison to the six million strong army that Russia, Britain's ally, could field, but unlike Russia's was world class in competence, largely through sustaining the empire for three centuries. The "Old Contemptibles" were in truth-seasoned professionals. Thus, despite Grey's pessimism, the mood at large was one of jingoistic optimism in Britain. Anti-War rhetoric was associated with the more activist and leftist elements of British life: Irish nationalists, suffragettes, Socialist groups, and anti-imperial elements in India. The justice of the war was broadly endorsed, and reinforced by fear-mongering and demonizing of "the Hun." Admittedly, the German march through Belgium did little to undermine that stereotype. The first signs of brutality were exhibited by German troops where they encountered civilian resistance. While stories of bayonetted babies were exaggerated, the reality was that hundreds of Belgian civilians, including women and children, were executed where the Germans encountered opposition. The mythologizing of the brutal Hun—portrayed as a King Kong-like figure with a spiked helmet—and justification for a total war mentality can be seen to take roots in the German invasion of Belgium.

The invasion itself was indeed ruthless and totalizing. Since the Schlieffen Plan required a rapid victory over France, the march through Belgium was relentless and extraordinary, as described by the American journalist Richard Harding Davis for his audience back in the US, as he sat in a sidewalk cafeteria and watched the invasion proceed through the capital, Brussels:

> For two hours I watched them, and then, bored with the monotony of it, returned to the hotel. After an hour, from beneath my window, I still could hear them; another hour and another went by. They still were passing.
>
> Boredom gave way to wonder. The thing fascinated you, against your will, dragged you back to the sidewalk and held you there open-eyed. No longer was it regiments of men marching, but something uncanny, inhuman, a force of nature like a landslide, a tidal wave, or lava sweeping down a mountain. It was not of this earth, but mysterious, ghostlike. It carried all the mystery and menace of a fog rolling toward you across the sea.
>
> The German army moved into Brussels as smoothly and as compactly as an Empire State express. There were no halts, no open places, no stragglers…
>
> All through the night, like a tumult of a river when it races between the cliffs of a canyon, in my sleep I could hear the steady roar of the passing army. And when early in the morning I went to the window the chain of steel was still unbroken…And for three

> days and three nights through Brussels it roared and rumbled, a cataract of molten lead. The infantry marched singing, with their iron-shod boots beating out the time. They sang Fatherland, My Fatherland. Between each line of song they took three steps. At times 2000 men were singing together in absolute rhythm and beat. It was like blows from giant pile-drivers. When the melody gave way the silence was broken only by the stamp of iron-shod boots, and then again the song rose. When the singing ceased the bands played marches. They were followed by the rumble of the howitzers, the creaking of wheels and of chains clanking against the cobblestones, and the sharp, bell-like voices of the bugles.
>
> When at night for an instant the machine halted, the silence awoke you, as at sea you wake when the screw stops.
>
> For three days and three nights the column of gray, with hundreds of thousands of bayonets and hundreds of thousands of lances, with gray transport wagons, gray ammunition carts, gray ambulances, gray cannon, like a river of steel, cut Brussels in two.[1]

The adapted Schlieffen Plan required each element to succeed, which unfortunately for Germany was not realized. The French army's ability to move north toward Belgium, and the surprising rapidity of Russian mobilization in the east meant that the goal of a six week victory for Germany was doomed from the start. Schlieffen had correctly concluded that knocking out France prior to Russia being ready was essential to a two-front

---

[1] Richard Harding Davis, *New York Tribune*, 23 August 1914.

War strategy for victory. By September the War had created a new dynamic, the March to the Sea, a term well known for different reasons in the America's South. In 1914 it meant that the French, with troops from Britain's Expeditionary Force, were racing northward as were the Germans to seal the North Sea ports and prevent each opposing army looping around the northern "top" and attacking from behind. The net result was the creation of a new front that soon developed into a 700 kilometer line from the North Sea to the Swiss Alps, the eponymous Western Front. The early months saw the opposing armies facing each other in grueling warfare. The Battles of Mons, the Marne, Aisne, The Race to the Sea and Antwerp are, among others, moments when history changed, with the realization that a defensive war would increasingly define the prosecution of the Great War. Moreover, with static armies facing each other with materiel and technology in proportions and ferocity unheard of previously, the question of defense was essential. Paradoxically, while technological innovation and new armaments provided the attacking strategy, the defensive necessity as a response prompted a timeless and prehistoric answer, as old as humankind, grounding war deep in the soil itself.

The establishment of a static front with men and materiel of colossal volume taught rapidly the need for security within soil. This principle had to some degree been learned in the American Civil War. But the scale of excavation in the Great War became its figurehead, namely trench warfare. Initially, during the autumn of 1914, the armies had faced each other using only rudimentary protection, such as shell holes, natural undulations, trees where available, and the debris of towns and war machinery. Such protection was patently inadequate for the ferocity of fighting that artillery, infantry, and cavalry faced in the second decade of the twentieth century. So, into an underground existence the opposing armies crawled, with an experience so defining and far-reaching that today we still employ within our vernacular phrases derived directly from the four years of winding trenches that millions of men literally disappeared into. "Digging in," "last ditch," "over the top," "no-man's-land," "let's bag it," "two's company, three's a crowd," "keep your head below the parapet" and others are each drawn from the Allied trenches of the 1914–18 War. The trenches were typically arranged in three rows, with an advance trench facing the enemy, a reserve trench behind it (for reserve and exchange troops), and a communications trench at the rear, to ensure communications from the rear guard positions and HQ were sent forward. Between these trenches ran connecting trench lines to "traffic" men, materiel, and messages back and forth. The front line advance trenches were directly facing across "no-man's-land," which was heavily fortified by all sides with barbed wire. At the closest on the Vimy Ridge of the Somme, the distance between opposing front line trenches was ten meters. More usually some hundreds of meters might need crossing to cover the terrain and reach the front line of the enemy's front trench.

The 700 kilometer front between the Alps and the North Sea turned into ten thousand actual kilometers of interlocking trenches. The trench systems became complex lines of living, combat, and endurance, usually patterned according to purpose. The front line trenches were designed in zig-zag directions, to prevent shell burst traveling the length of the trench and to defend positions easier. In these trenches, bunkers were constructed, often elaborately and deep underground, with greater comforts being provided for officers. The walls of trenches were initially built with sandbags and pallets of wood. Later, they were filled by design and consequences of battle with corpses, body parts, and debris. At the top of the trench, at heights of between five and nine feet, were the parapets, wooden sides with access points for leaping out or "going over the top." The trench frontier ran through some of the lowest and saturated soil on earth. The clay soils of Flanders, the low lying terrain, and the drained rivers that had irrigated local agriculture, ensured that a trench bottom was often submerged and filled up rapidly with water. The infamous condition of trench foot was the result of weeks of standing knee high in filthy, infected, louse-ridden, rat-carrying mud and water. The standard duckboard on the floor of the front line trench did something to mitigate circumstances, as did the constant pumping of water, but nothing could beat the odds of evading a hell of mud and water, both in the trench and the shell-pocked "no-man's-land" that was a literal sea of corpses and debris. In this trench the ordinary British soldier (nicknamed a "Tommy") carried the standard weapons of the day: a knife, perhaps a bomb (grenade) and the bolt-action Lee Enfield rife complete with bayonet, the latter being the most common. This was the equipment that the British soldier typically carried into war and across no-man's-land in the face of the "The Devil's Paintbrush," or the machine guns that were emplaced in enemy "nests" that could cover every foot of no-man's-land. Given the inequity of rifle and machine gun, the result was a near certain death trap in setting foot into no-man's-land. The math illustrated the deadly inequity well. At 800 yards, a machine gun could destroy an invading force fourteen times larger than the defenders. For a rifle to do similar, the enemy would need to be 200 yards from the defenders with equal numbers of men facing each other. In this environment, the death zone was inevitable and usually impenetrable.

The diary of Private R. A. Colwell from January 1918, after the infamous Second Battle of Ypres (or Passchendaele), describes the ominous nihilism of no-man's-land confronting the soldiers and their fate: "There was not a sign of life of any sort. Not a tree, save for a few dead stumps which looked strange in the moonlight. Not a bird, not even a rat or a blade of grass. Nature was as dead there as those Canadians whose bodies remained where they had fallen the previous autumn. Death was written large everywhere."[2]

The trenches behind the front line were slightly more inhabitable, since the one-stage removal of direct conflict and the ability to repair easier ensured slightly better maintenance. Behind the second row of reserve trenches was the third communications trench, which intentionally needed to be utilized expeditiously and efficiently to ensure the messages were sent, received and responded. The emergence of trench warfare led to an extraordinary development in surveying and mapping, with which Lewis Blake would have been intimately connected. At War's outbreak the British and French used Michelin road maps to guide their territorial strategy. By War's conclusion over thirty million trench maps had been produced and every British army had its own Field Survey Battalion, drawn from the Royal Engineers. The necessity of trench mapping was to ensure both accurate knowledge of one's own trenches and military placements (e.g. dug-outs, machine gun nests, barbed wire) and more importantly to track via both air and ground reconnaissance the changing entrenchments of the enemy. To add an element of familiarity, trenches and land-marks were given names that resembled streets and places back home: Hellfire Corner; Old Kent Road; King's Arms Pub; Rats Alley, among hundreds of examples. For Lewis, as an artillery gunner and runner, famil-

[2] Poster Exhibit at National Infantry Museum, Fort Benning, Georgia.

iarity with maps was essential work since the British artillery used an elaborate grid system to identify numeric coordinates in determining shelling strategy. The grids were a mathematical overlay that stayed constant, while the specific trench and land features would move and vary over the four years of conflict.

One of the staggering realizations was that only a few kilometers behind the front lines, life and environment could appear intact, particularly on the Allied side where no enemy Army of Occupation was present. Villages could function with the appearance of normal life and on the Allied territory without destruction. For the Allied territories, the armies were welcome saviors, comrades and customers for all needs, including physical satisfaction and relief. On the German side, the Belgian inhabitants were occupied, and had to deal with the ambiguities facing all occupied citizens, especially those who had received harsh and vicious treatment at the hands of the German army in its punishing march through Belgium. That German army was by year's end preparing for a long stay. The Schlieffen Plan had no concept of what to do if the invading German force was held at bay. The German Generals, and especially Hindenberg and von Falkenhayn, realized quickly that they already had now gained occupied territory, and that the Allies were thus in the political disadvantage. While Sir John French, commander of the British Expeditionary Force, and later his replacement the Earl Douglas Haig, considered it unimaginable not to press and attack, the

German strategy embraced defense, thus making even more permanent the notion of a trench front that was static. That reality impelled the Germans by early 1915 to begin construction of deep concrete bunkers within their trench systems. They established an entire subterranean system of living and exhibited a determination to hold out for the long run.

Such thinking was anathema to the Allies who thus failed to reinforce their trench system with the same diligence as the Germans, contributing to the misery of the living conditions for their front line soldiers. Of course each side continued to believe in the eventual success of a "big push" that would finally break the deadlock and see its victorious army move toward capture of Berlin or Paris respectively. The four years of the War expended millions of lives in what effectively became both a war of attrition (a "last man standing" view of victory) and also a war of decision (a "great breakthrough" view of victory). It is also important to note that the War did indeed see the line moving, often a few kilometers, and occasionally more drastically, such as in the Spring Offensive by the Germans in 1918. But, as historians, poets, novelists, and artists have so effectively conveyed across the generations, the reality of the Western Front was a living hell of human suffering stuck in the mud for four years, with little chance of movement, little chance of change and a great chance of premature death in a manner so horrific that the imagination struggles to conjure or cope with that likelihood.

All that formally and officially documents my grandfather's role and presence in this reality is his military service card, recorded in the British National Archives and now available for online research. Alongside the two million Britons who served, and millions of other Empire troops, a few lines on his military card note that Blake, Lewis was assigned to the RFA (Royal Field Artillery), with the rank of Gunner and the Regimental designation of L/828.[3] The card is all that remains of a young life, alongside millions, who shaped history and my family ever more. Intriguingly, the two words "rank amended" are penned there too, with "enclo 5a" as a descriptor. Gunner Blake's War was official and certified business, and history bequeaths and records his designation as a soldier of the Great War. If Flanders showed him chaos and death, it is of some poetic justice that his yard became a place where earth and soil could allow his later years to create order, beauty, and peace.

[3] Noted on p.372 of Catalog RFA/102B, National Archives of the UK (TNA).

4.

A Bombardier's Testament of Youth

Erich Maria Remarque, a German veteran on the War, published in 1928 possibly the most famous anti-war novel of all time, *All Quiet on the Western Front* (*Im Westen nichts Neues*). It captured supremely the sentiment and experience of a generation that endured the unimaginable. Its protest of the War was equally mirrored for posterity in the poetry of the First World War. In the voice of the poet and author belonged a prophet-like expression of human experience and suffering that historical detail and strategic explanation would fail to convey. Eleven years prior to Remarque's publication the *London Times* in the summer of 1917 had published Siegfried Sassoon's *Letter of Protest*. Despite being a remarkable and Military Cross decorated officer of the Royal Welsh Fusiliers, known as Mad Jack for his willingness to go into no-man's-land to retrieve the wounded, Sassoon famously brought to the world in his story, his poetry and his public letter the voice of protest from the men who were being led to slaughter. Like those men, Sassoon was conflicted about the need for the War, aware of both its senseless and devastating nature, and also admitting to the need to combat Teutonic aggression, as he later journaled. His letter of July 1917 brought to the public the argument that "the war is being deliberately prolonged by those who have the power to end it... I can no longer be party to prolong those sufferings for ends which I believe to be evil and unjust."[1]

The phrase "all quiet on the western front" refers to the response of the German HQ to Berlin, stationed a few kilometers behind its front trench, at the eleventh hour of the eleventh day of the eleventh month of 1918. It signaled that the armistice, signed six hours earlier in railway carriage number 2491D in the forest of Compiegne, had held intact, though tested until the eleventh hour literally, and that the guns were now finally silent. Lewis Blake was on that front when the phrase was first a reality before it became a legend. He was a soldier who had been there, and now was soon to start a new life in which the Great War was his autobiography but, thankfully, not his demise. Four years earlier it was part of a much younger Lewis Blake's baptism into adulthood as well. His skills as a young man were relevant in the birth of the so-called War to End All Wars, in the context of life's tale that is both faintly charming and horrifyingly tragic. Lewis had been one of eight children, the third from youngest, and his father was a horticultural merchant specializing in flora. At the start of the century he had been living in Sandy, north of London. During his childhood he had developed horse-handling skills, by virtue of his Uncle Henry who owned a farm a short

[1] Gary Sheffield, *The First World War in 100 Objects* (London Andre Deutsch Ltd., 2013) 183.

train ride away and had used Lewis as a boy hand to assist with the horses. This skill was to provc beneficial to the family business both in rural Sandy and then in Mitcham, south London, where his father moved the family to build his business. Horse-traffic in London in 1900 moved at an average speed of eleven miles per hour, only two miles per hour slower than automotive traffic in the Capital city one hundred years later. Suffice to say that horsemanship was valued greatly, not only by the aristocracy as the sport of kings, but among the mercantile classes who moved goods and business by rail or by horse. Lewis Blake grew to be a boy who could handle a horse as best as anyone his father knew. By the age of fourteen he was working for a large warehousing firm, Fairbrothers, through the assistance of his scout master, giving young Lewis his first experience in what today is known as business logistics. Fairbrothers realized the value of his horse-handling and he was rapidly given responsibilities of horse care and deliveries around an area of south London. This was the context to my grandfather's teen years and his budding career when the great imperial nations of the nineteenth century hurtled headlong toward self-destruction in the early twentieth century.

When the recruiting officer told sixteen-year old Lewis to walk around the block and consider carefully a revised birth year, he wasn't simply responding to the need for numbers. He would, as my grandfather would recall later, be recruited for his horsemanship more than any other skill. While Salisbury Plain boot camp would have taught his basic training, it was horsemanship that would define his career and potentially save his life. We rightly remember and mourn the ten million men who died in the Great War. What we hardly notice are the staggering eight million horses that died in the same conflict, experiences both my grandfathers were to witness at first hand for 4 years.

For Lewis Blake, his horsemanship was a prize too important to wait for enlistment regulations on minimum age. He enlisted in the artillery, since his skills on London's streets had been in moving merchandise in a pressured environment with the assistance of horses. The Western Front was to play out varied scenarios repeatedly over its four years and four months, in which artillery, and its constant maneuvering, was only possible through enormous use of horse transportation. The use of artillery involved pre-planned integration with infantry actions, especially in the reliance of the artillery barrage as a pre-cursor to the ground infantry advance, and later in the "creeping barrage," which relied on a curtain of advancing friendly fire behind which the infantry would move forward. This meant that horses were used to position the guns, move them during action to new positions, and do so under desperate conditions. The extent of that desperate nature can be gleaned in the length of the barrage. In the week prior to the Battle of the Somme seven days of continuous artillery barrage was ranged on the German lines, with the belief they would be obliterated ahead of the advancing British infantry expecting devastated enemy trenches upon arrival. Two years later, during the German Spring Offensive of 1918, the Germans launched one million shells in advance of their move. Total artillery shell count on all sides of the Great War produced a billion shells, of which 15% never exploded. A harvest of metal still takes place annually when plowed fields spew forth vast quantities of unexploded ordnance. Flemish farmers to this day leave this deadly harvest by their road sides, and it is collected by the local military bomb squad on a routine basis for disposal.

This explosion of the sky, as it was commonly described by the soldiers in the field, required a massive amount of artillery, gunners, and horses. This is why bombardier Blake was worth admitting underage into the volunteer army in the autumn of 1914, and why by January he had traveled the mere ten hours by rail and sea to northern France. His horsemanship was to prove invaluable as an artilleryman in two distinct ways.

Firstly, it meant that he knew how to deliver artillery cannon to the sites that became ever more important as the trench lines of the Western Front solidified. In this defensive war the role of artillery was to remain the first and foremost memory of soldiers, and the signal of an infantry advance. Images abound of artillery production across Europe, giving many women their first experience of paid employment. Today artillery shell cases can be bought for a few euros all over antique shops in northern Europe, and continue to be exhumed daily. Lewis Blake was one of tens of thousands of bombardiers whose job was to deliver the nearly billion shells fired in the Great War to their final deadly destination.

The scale and nature of that artillery experience is familiar to us a century later through the catalogs of diaries, memoirs, archival research, documentary analysis, scholarly works and fiction, both written and filmed. To the lost generation of 1914-18 this though was the frontier of human experience, unknown and unimagined to all combatants in preceding history. No reference point, no speculation, no previous war history, no training on Salisbury Downs could prepare "Tommy Atkins," or Lewis Blake, for the enormity of that alignment of warfare and industrialization. It simply exploded—figuratively and literally—onto the human landscape in a manner so enormous and unfamiliar that to every combatant it exposed a side of life that could not be fully conceptualized or contained. Lewis Blake was thrust into this new kind of warfare with names that history has memorialized—the Somme, Arras, Champagne—but to him and his Tommy comrades it was real, sensual, speechless and awful: a theatre of living hell and absurd suffering. My grandfather's work and that of his comrades was observed by a Royal Flying Corps memoir from April 1917, written by Billy Bishop who was flying over the Battle of Arras:

> The shell fire this morning was simply indescribable...The British barrage fire that morning was

> the most intense the war had ever known. There was greater concentration of guns than at any time during the Somme...The waves of attacking infantry as they came out of their trenches and trudged forward behind the curtain of shells laid down by the artillery were an amazing sight. The men seemed to wander across No Man's Land, and into the enemy trenches, as if the battle was a great bore to them. From the air it looked like they did not realize that they were at war and were taking it all too quietly. That is the way with clockwork warfare....To me it seemed that they must soon wake up and run; that they were altogether too slow; that they could not realize the great danger they were in. .. Nor could I believe that the little brown figures moving about below me were really men—men going to the glory of victory or to the glory of death. I could not make myself realize the full truth or meaning of it all. It all seemed that I was in an entirely different world, looking down from another sphere on this strange, uncanny puppet-show. And the battle, so calmly entered into, was one of the tensest, bitterest of the entire world war.[2]

This reality was one that my grandfather helped create and sustain. How it changed him, his soul and his life was to remain essentially between him and his God. All we know from our vantage point of history is that the boy who worked in fields of flowers with his horse was to become the young man whose horse was his war asset in new fields of blood and steel.

---

[2] Jon E. Lewis, ed. *A Brief History of World War I* (London: Robinson & Running Press, 2014) 293.

Secondly, his horsemanship also gave him an additional singularly distinct role, beyond that of Gunner and horsemanship. Communications in the First World War evolved into a sophisticated and essential strategy for the battles being waged. For the artillery, the emergence of the creeping barrage is perhaps one of the best illustrations. At the start of the war, the role of artillery was to pound enemy lines, in order to ease the infantry attack across no-man's-land. When tens of thousands of infantrymen walked into a hail of machine gun fire or, surviving that, arrived at an intact trench manned still with enemy soldiers, it was obvious that the barrage itself was insufficient to protect the foot soldiers. Hence the development of the "creeping barrage," providing a screen of protection merely yards in front of the marching infantry, to give direct protection and enable the infantry to move closer to the enemy. Such an integrated tactic of combining the efforts of artillery and infantry, deadly in terms of "friendly fire" if miscalculated, required extraordinary integration and collaboration. The key was a two-way communications between HQ and field stations for both artillery and infantry. Unfortunately, phone and radio apparatus was frequently destroyed by the shelling. Runners were often used (the 1981 movie "Gallipoli" highlights this), but limited in distance and subject to the sniper's cross-hairs. Horseback riding provided an improved solution. The theatrical West End play, *War Horse*,[3] draws attention similarly

---

[3] *War Horse*, the play by Michael Morpurgo.

to the extraordinary stamina and value of horses. And in this respect, Lewis Blake's skills presented a symbiosis of man and animal in a way that the Great War captured to a new level.

The communications needs between trenches required constant mobility of message and man, and Corporal Blake was one of a few in his section tasked with riding between HQ some kilometers behind lines, artillery positions nearer the front, and the front itself. To do this would clearly risk man and horse. To succeed in doing this for four years seems extraordinary. However, the undertaking gave him a unique perspective on the three angles of the conflict, and enabled him to communicate official messages while building networks between the men at their various postings. Later in the War, communications reached its zenith most ironically in the use of the homing pigeon, birds trained to send and retrieve paper messages attached by a metal band to their legs. The French had remembered the effective used of pigeons in the siege of Paris during the Franco-Prussian War some forty years earlier and had reinstated the use as early as the Battle of the Marne in 1914, but still the belief in progress and science limited its early embrace. This centuries' old method of communicating was initially dismissed by generals on all sides in an age of advanced technology.

The siege of Verdun in 1916, one of history's most appalling and costly battles, changed that. The French major tasked with the defense of Fort Vaux issued his final desperate message via a homing pigeon, which on reaching its intended allies then succumbed to the effects of gas and bullet and expired. It is now celebrated with a posthumous Legion of Honor and kept as a stuffed memorial in a museum, and inspired thousands of postcards during the War depicting the brave French Major sending forth the pigeon like Noah over an endless ocean. Northern English soldiers had brought to the Front their skills in the raising of homing pigeons as a hobby, a hobby that transformed war communications. It is estimated that homing pigeons had a ninety percent success rate. They were so successful that in the autumn of 1917 the Germans realized the Allies were relying on this ancient method of communications, and imported Falcons from Prussia to hunt down the Allied pigeons. The U.S. also imported pigeons upon joining the War in 1917, and one of the U.S. Marines's most celebrated heroes was "Cher Ami," a homing pigeon that was shot by Germans, lost a leg, and still managed to complete its mission and survive. It was given a hero's departure by General Pershing himself, and awarded the *Croix de Guerre* by the grateful French.

Until that ninety percent success rate was understood, soldiers like Lewis Blake and other communications runner needed to execute missions of communications, as well as deliver artillery. In this respect, the movie and play *War Horse* provided a powerful illustration of the terrible conditions that he endured as a communications runner in the four years he served. The rate of casualties for animals was as extraordinary as the amount of livestock that was exported to France and other global places of conflict, to support the troops in service or nutritionally. We do know some stories from Lewis that resonated across the years, thought doubtless many more were kept private to him. Firstly, in traveling between HQ and the artillery and trench positions, he became well known to officers and enlisted men. As a result he was asked to transport messages and material, such as Woodbine cigarettes in packs of ten. The simple exchange of gifts, goods and small comforts became something he would facilitate. And for soldiers at the Front, the extraordinary need and satisfaction of simple comforts, whether occasional fruitcake and liquor from home, or tea and cigarettes on a daily basis, cannot be overstated. This was where the Salvation Army provided a core service to the men in the trenches, ensuring a steady supply of highly valued commodities at small distribution huts near the front. As the Confederate Army yearned for coffee in the American Civil War, so the Tommies in France sixty years later yearned for "tea and Woodbines," a phrase often said that won the War for the Allies. Cigarettes were often distributed for free, and when not readily available immediately traded within the trenches. "Woodbine Willie," named originally after a chaplain who went out his way to ensure troops had their "tea and Woodbines," became a term of endearment when someone, like Lewis, could help in their procurement. Interestingly, another tradition that emerged from this trench life of a more sinister nature is the superstition that one must never light more than two cigarettes from a single lit match. Rapidly the troops learned from bitter experience that at night the light from a match would reveal to an enemy sniper the location of a soldier and specifically his head. By the time the third cigarette was lit, the sniper had sufficient time to load, aim and fire, and the third smoker was thus the mortal victim. That brutal experience still today teaches British smokers never to light more than two cigarettes with one match.

When Lewis Blake did not have exact money change for the exchange of cigarettes, tea and other goods, though, it got him into trouble with the officers. Though he was simply acting as a "creditor" for a day or two, it was judged by his superiors that he was illegally trading with the troops for profit, a punishable offence. At that point Corporal Blake was disciplined by the removal of his Corporal's stripes and being demoted to the ranks. That clearly hurt his sense of pride and justice, but fortunately for Lewis it was a short-lived punishment. Some weeks later, he was running a communication to the trenches, when on pulling back the canvas cover of a trench dug-out, the incoming oxygen re-ignited the hessian fabric on the sandbags. The engulfing flames spread up the sandbags and threatened to ignite a general trench fire. Reacting on impulse, he snuffed out the flames with his hands and arms, successfully extinguishing the fire but incurring some bad burns to both his hands. This act earned him back immediately his Corporal's stripes, which he maintained until war's ends. It is that act to which the two words "rank amended" on his archived military card give testimony. His recounting of this story is known in our family for decades, and recorded for posterity in the notes of his military record card.

Lewis Blake's War experiences were communicated in anecdote. One can only speculate on the nature of his deeper memories of the War for surely the four years in France were infinitely larger than anecdote, in every sense. Yet, in a way, these fragments give clue in a way that conventional history may overlook. Lewis fought and lived through some of the most gruesome battles of human history, from the age of seventeen to twenty. We know from his familiarity with certain towns—Bapaume, Albert, Ypres—that he was a gunner and runner at the battles of Second Ypres and the Somme. These two battles live in the infamy of War. Their details not needing restating here, since the volumes available on the magnitude and originality of their suffering are abundant. How Lewis made sense of, say, the first day of the Somme, is unknown. How does a person conceptualize the costliest day in casualties in British history, when 20,000 died and another 40,000 were hideously injured in a fifteen hour span? What we know is that he could recall some experiences that touched his heart and soul. That he shared with me that on his 17th birthday he and another Tommy were searching a farm near no-man's-land for eggs and had drifted from the lines. Suddenly they encountered some yards away two German soldiers doing similar, and each pair desperately discharged their firearms and ran away in fear. That same birthday of 24 January he recounted his first experience of incoming enemy artillery. Why he would choose to share that, and not an abundance of examples from the four years of inconceivably huge artillery action and response cannot be evaluated. What I surmise is that what we describe as trivia in a day is perhaps the way our identity responds to living events. When pressed once by me on the subject of the War I saw an angry side of my grandfather that I never saw again. I naively and insensitively suggested he had experienced as a combatant the kind of life few of us ever had the chance to experience. Angrily he snapped back at me: "What are you talking about? The lucky ones were the ones who never came home." That was his only reference ever in anger, and I learned not to ask again. Only with the passing of years did I begin to get a sense of what that desperate remark might convey both about both my grandfather and the cataclysm of a lost generation one hundred years ago.

So, Lewis Blake recounted relatively few other memories. Aside from his time joining the War, his main other focus was upon its end. He took great pleasure, with vivid laughter and mimicking of his comrades, at their attempt to raise those sunken "petit bateaux" at the bottom of a canal. Presumably they did so out of boredom, which is a major recurrent theme from soldiers' journals about the war of their experiences of endless days of boredom followed by dreadful action. He would speak often and fondly about Old Joe, the cook, whom he feared and respected but who clearly showed paternalistic interest in his teenage soldiers. He would also talk about logistics and practical requirements. Ridding oneself of lice was a constant demand, but he repeatedly told me that Jeyes Fluid, a powerful antiseptic, was too corrosive of the skin. He laughed voraciously once when he told me that he and a young pal poured it over their genitalia to get rid of the lice, only to give the other troops a comedic show as they danced around in agony until they could wash it off. The egalitarian nature of louse infection meant all ranks would find that lice would return as quickly as you could destroy them by crushing them between fingernails. Estimates are that troops would spend one waking hour each day trying to remove lice, to little permanent avail. For my grandfather, this anecdote was indicative of his detailed observations about trench horrors and experiences. In the same breath he would talk negatively about the French, his allies, and admiringly about the Germans, his adversaries. The Germans "got the job done," whereas the French were always difficult.

This perspective of war is revealing: a form of social history, embedded with personal narrative. It frustrated me that Lewis Blake did not serialize or conceptualize his "history of the Somme," until I realized that his history was what he chose to memorialize, and not my presupposition about the Somme's importance. It is essential that we allow that personal narrative to inform the larger historical one, for not only does it show us a human face of history, but as just importantly tells us each about our own ancestral traditions that have molded us. For example, Lewis Blake did not tell me about the extent of the death, injury, suffering, and inhumanity he witnessed as a young man. He did not tell me what he thought about his extinguishing the lives of countless men in Flanders in the tens of thousands of artillery shells he fired. He did not tell me what he saw in the putrid trenches and hellish field hospitals where he was expected to take communication messages. He did not tell me what the "sound of the sky" was like when a week of continuous shelling preceded the fated going "over the top" on the first day of the Somme. He did not tell me which comrades he saw blown apart, and which ones he missed desperately. And why should he? That legacy, bequeathed as a new horror by the Great War, was part of a story which he inhabited but chose not to dwell within. Instead, he remembered old Joe the cook. Instead, he remembered the laughter on that cold December day in 1918 in trying to get the boat out the water. Instead, he grimly remembered being told to shoot his horse, Satan, because it had no longer had any use, even though it had carried him for years in the killing fields of Flanders, alongside the other million horses that the British took to France. Instead, Lewis Blake liked to laugh and loudly bark the words "Fall In" when he saw me, repeating the military call to attention when moving forward, or recalling from his "boot camp" experience on Salisbury Plain of falling into drill formation, long marching, use of a trench spade, and practice bayonetting on a bag. Later Lewis would have been introduced to the distinctive British pick-axe in the trenches, which became for his generation the standard gardening tool for the rest of their lives. Lewis's pick-axe is still hanging up in my father's garage.

Lewis Blake, or Pops, could tell me about the leather oils he used to soften the straps on his horses, the ointments that worked well with the wounds in man and beasts, and the tedium of bully beef and the constant search for pigs and chickens to vary the diet. He would have been familiar on a daily basis with the ordnance of destruction, especially with the handling and firing of thousands of artillery shells and "Mills Bomb No. 5" hand grenades. In the summer of 1916, in the region where Pops served near Pozieres and the Somme, some 73,000 hand-grenades were launched by the British. Much of their usage was in the close combat environment of trench assault and defense, and especially in moving between front, communications and rear trenches, the very terrain he was responsible for covering as a communications runner. What he witnessed is accounted for in the many annals of historical texts, but not recorded by Lewis himself.

Instead, fortune allowed him not to have to express in too much detail what history tells us about the mud, death, torture, and carnage that was the Western Front. My grandfather lived and fought at an age that was extraordinarily young and inconceivably cruel. And he made sense of that in a way that worked for the remainder of his long life. For despite the cruelty, the human dimension provided him a means of recounting the value of life and company. After the War, while the British were gathering at St. Omer to organize their return home, a friend of his Jack Brandon was about to return to England but had no work prospects. On learning that a new London passport office was opening to accommodate anticipated war refugees, Lewis Blake was able to ride several kilometers to pass on the news to his friend, Jack. Jack used his short leave to obtain future work, and a career in public administration, as a result. He was proud to relay that story, that illustration of human help, and optimism. For him, the Great War was remembered and expressed in those terms of the human spirit and not in the desperation and sorrow that it wrought upon the Forgotten Generation and its loved ones.

Indeed, my conviction is that Lewis Blake reconciled his war experiences in a way that empowered his life's progress. For Lewis, his chosen memories gave him a framework for living in the hope of the future. His home embodied an emblem and symbol of a world put back into order from chaos, into sublimation from annihilation, into productivity from destruction, into the hope of age from the decimation of youth. From a landscape of trenches full of water, blood, and the stench of death, and an annihilated no-man's-land stretched endlessly and violently forward. That landscape was sublimated instead into the tender care of a garden of beauty, where nature blossomed and grass grew and order thrived. Where once artillery shell pounded earth into a myriad water-logged shell holes and evaporated men by the hundreds of thousands, now his home was one where garden bowls, not shells, could be thrown gently and competed over for victory. Where once the elements of northern Europe froze and drenched and steamed the armies facing each other, freezing to death the armies of Austro-Hungary in their absurd Carpathian winter campaigns, or giving trench foot to the armies of Britain and France standing for weeks in mud up to their knees, or dying of thirst and dysentery to the armies of Australia and New Zealand as they clung to cliff ledges in the futile summer months on the Gallipoli peninsula. Where once nature, as well as man, was a mortal and relentless enemy, Lewis Blake's home now embraced and befriended nature, an enemy no longer. And where the poppy once grew by the billions across the scarred face of Flanders in the spring of 1919, after the artillery shells no longer rained down, the red poppy of the honored fallen millions now could now be replaced in Lewis's life by a red geranium. A red geranium that could express beauty and life and not a poppy that memorialized suffering. A geranium that symbolized life rather than the poppy that grew out of a land made fertile with the corpses of the fallen.

Yet at the ends of Lewis Blake's home, the symbols of a past upheaval were not far away. Surely that past lurked throughout his long life and close to his memories. Lewis returned, married my grandmother Lydia, ran a successful family business supporting the shoe industry, fathered four children with Lydia, and survived the Great Depression and the rest of the century's stresses, public and private. His home was one where grandchildren observed a successful and happy life in order. But at its edges the making of his memory was not far away, and I imagine he never forgot. At the end of his garden, behind the hedge, the twisted iron and steel of his gardening equipment resembled the destroyed machines of war that he so intimately managed. The stream at his garden's rear was a bordering trench that he rarely visited, since he had so frequently visited so many trenches as a young man. And, in the darkest and deepest corner of his attic, he still could not take it upon himself to have removed, until his death and its subsequent house clearance, a box of pineapple-shaped Mills No. 5 hand grenades that had oddly come back from the War as a souvenir to its pained experiences. I cannot accept, nor do I believe in retrospect, that he actually believed that the lucky ones were the ones who never came back. But I do believe that those who did come back had the scars of injustice and the challenge of learning to build lives that could find healing from wounds, hope from despair, order from chaos, and humanity from hatred.

5.

Once More unto the Breach, Dear Friends

Horace Holbrook Wood died of lung disease (as noted earlier) decades after becoming a mustard gas victim of combat in World War I. His life thus illustrates that the War's effects, personally, locally and globally, bore an enduring trajectory through the twentieth century. I knew him simply as a toddler with a solitary memory of his lap blanket and so had no depth of personal relationship with him as a grandfather. But my sense of connection to him has grown throughout my life, largely in part due to a remark he made, perhaps at that same moment that I can recall, to my mother and father, namely, "I have to get better to watch this one grow up." That loving but futile comment speaks of the each generation's hope to connect with the past and future, and that family genealogy is our primary motivator and opportunity to achieve that. So fragments of knowledge about Grandfather Horace have always reminded me of that wish, an alternative to a *Nunc Dimittis* resignation and instead a burning and enduring hope, even as his lungs were expiring. Ironically, the enduring image of Horace is a headshot black and white photograph of a smiling man in his fifties with pipe in mouth. If ever the incongruity of medical and personal conditions were evident, that photo says it all. Yet the Tommies (and Fritzes) of the Great War were the consumers of tobacco like no other generation, and had less problems with incompatible lifestyle choices than later self-absorbed, greater-informed generations.

Family lore had communicated an outline of Horace's war career that was referenced earlier. It was powerful and patchy, the former in its personal intimacies of his friendship and marriage during and after the War, the latter in its lack of military detail. In the writing of this book, though, new detail emerged that shed further light on his War experiences and their effect on his life. In obtaining his military service card via online registration with the U.K. National Archives, it was clear that Horace was not, as thought by my mother and likely my grandmother too, a service Cavalry soldier, but in fact a Mounted Infantry soldier. This was new information that meant that for decades his military service was understood incorrectly by my family. Aside from the interesting coincidence that both my grandfathers experienced the War with equine dependency, Horace's role was that of a specific infantry function that relied on horses, honored in the story of Charge of the Light Brigade in the Crimean War, concluding in World War Two when horses were abandoned as a front line asset. There is only one Horace H. Wood in British military record, with a regimental number of 119672 in the Nottingham and Derbyshire Regiment (the "Sherwood Foresters," of Robin Hood legendary fame), and his record, like Lewis Blake's also, notes that his war service was awarded the standard Victory medal and British Warrior medal after de-mobilization.

He could have been sent to Mesopotamia with other mounted infantry of his regiment, but instead went with millions of his young compatriots to Flanders Fields. Unlike Lewis's stories, which record his engagement, we know little of Horace's battle details. But the "Light Horseman" brigades, as commonly described, were well known in the British, Australian, and New Zealand armies, heroically mythologized in the Charge of the Light Brigade. By World War I the charge of Crimea had been usurped by a less romanticized function. Historically known as Dragoons, by the 1914–18 War the Light Infantry were no longer repeating Cavalry style-charges against enemy lines, but were combining horsemanship, often for transportation, with standard infantry style assault. This did allow them to carry more equipment and arms than traditional Cavalrymen or infantrymen. Their flexibility persuaded the Allies to deploy them variedly, illustrated in the 1987 movie *The Light Horseman* which recounts the Allied campaign in Sinai-Palestine and the Anzac 4th and 12th mounted infantry in the Battle of Beersheba, of October 1917. The journal of a British officer on the Somme records on 14 July 1916 the kind of fate that faced the attacking mounted infantry: "They were falling all the way as the

German (machine) guns played on the infantry. They simply galloped all through that, horses and men dropping with no hope against the machine guns. It was a magnificent sight. Tragic."[1]

Horace was thus a soldier of a military strategy that after centuries of use became, along with the regular horse Cavalry, dangerously obsolete with the advent of industrial warfare. Horace's service is part of a great watershed from which the Great War takes it identity as the tragic clashing of the old and new, and its catastrophic results that propelled a new military strategy. Yet the intimacy and endurance of the horse remained one of the treasured memories of old veterans, stories recounted for lifetimes of the care and security gleaned from this ancient animal of human affection. Although the Manfred Von Richthofen—"The Red Baron"—is remembered for his brilliant and deadly airmanship, Richthofen himself treasured his memories as a Lieutenant in the German mounted infantry at War's start, prior to his famed aviation career. His memoir details the same sense of flexibility, intimate partnership, and danger that man and horse knew uniquely in the Great War. Richthofen's Uhlan 1 Regiment, during the invasion of Belgium, encountered a French mounted infantry division by a forest near Etalle. Richthofen records their being ambushed and needing to retreat:

---

[1] Exhibit display, National Infantry Museum, Fort Benning, Georgia.

> To take cover was useless; therefore I had to go back. I was the last one. In spite of my orders, all the others had bunched together and offered the Frenchmen a good target. Perhaps that was the reason why I escaped. I brought only four men back. This baptism of fire was not as much fun as I thought. That evening some of the others came back, although they had to come by foot, as their horses were dead. It was really a miracle that nothing happened to me or my horse. The same night I was sent to Virton but did not get there as that town was taken by the enemy.[2]

The peculiar relationship between soldier and horse is legend from the Great War, and perhaps one of the most compelling examples, also now mythologized, is that of Simpson's Donkey from the disastrous and costly Gallipoli campaign of 1915. The story shows well the adaptive capacity of narrative, to change and reinforce different ideas, so much so that the historical reality is separate from the narrative message. In the cynical arena of politics, we now call that "post-truth" or "fake news". A kinder title and usage might be legend or myth. But the core of the Simpson story is his donkey (named both "Murphy" and "Duffy") and his work with the stretcher-bearer "Simpson" (actually John Simpson Kilpatrick) of an Australian field ambulance regiment and their rescuing of 300 wounded soldiers from the beaches and cliffs in the conflict. Simpson and his donkey are memorialized now in a striking bronze sculpture outside the Australian War Memorial in the capital city of Canberra,

[2] Lewis, *A Brief History of World War I,* 430.

exhibited for generations of school students.[3] The tale they learn of the donkey, and its connection to the tragic failure and legend of Gallipoli that resonates so strongly in Anzac history, continues to fuel our remembrance narrative of the Great War. That question we shall revisit at this book's conclusion but for now it is worth noting that the remembrance of the War is as cloudy as the fog of war itself, where sights, sounds and voices are open to confusion. Simpson, the actual man, was a North-Eastern Englishman, a Newcastle "Geordie," but the Australian legend and its enduring power maintains him as an "Aussie" with a donkey who epitomized national heroism.

What is indisputable is the military value the horse brought to the conflict, even in the twilight of its military career. Until the horse's sunset was complete by World War Two, the combating nations would view the horse as an integral asset and threat to all sides. The diary of a U-Boat captain, Adolf K.G.E. von Spiegel, who sank a steamer brining troops, arms and horses across the Atlantic in spring 1916, is telling:

> I saw (through the periscope), with surprise and shudder, long rows of wooden partitions right along all the decks, from which gleamed the shining black and brown back of horses. "Oh, heavens, horses! What a pity, those lovely beasts! But it cannot be helped," I went on thinking. "War is war, and every horse the fewer on the Western front is a reduction

---

[3] Sheffield, *The First World War in 100 Objects,* 29-30.

> of England's fighting power....Then, a second explosion, followed by the escape of white hissing steam....The white steam drove the horses made. I saw a beautiful long-tailed dapple-grey horse take a mighty leap over the berthing rails and land into a fully laden boat. At that point I could not bear the sight any longer, and I lowered the periscope and dived deep.[4]

The poignancy of horse and animal use in the Great War is an enduring theme of the sacrifice of the innocents, and one directly connected to the experience of both my grandfathers. For them, their War relied on equine companions. The danger of this romantic perception is that it risks masking the greater poignancy and loss of innocence, that of the human element. In the case of both Lewis and Horace, and like hundreds of thousands of others, this needs casting into the context of child-soldiers. The passion and naivety that could motivate sophisticated and civilized nations to send underage soldiers into a quagmire of shell and bullet is a loss of innocence that ripped childhood away from a complete generation. I look at my own two sons today, both in their early twenties, with inconceivable shock that they have reached ages that represented my grandfathers' returns as veterans of the War. That first month of August 1914 poured excitement and patriotism into a crucible of jingoistic fervor that spread like contagion across Europe. The British recruitment stations even provided

[4] Lewis, *A Brief History of World War I*, 184.

recruitment officers with bonuses for enhanced numbers, so the officer who told Lewis to walk around the block and return with a different age was not only filling trenches with more soldiers but filling his salary envelope with more shillings too. A cemetery outside of Ypres records the name of John Condon, killed in May 1915 at the Second Battle of Ypres, as possibly the youngest Allied soldier killed at the age of fourteen. More shocking is the enormous German cemetery a few kilometers away at Langemark, where 44,000 Germans are buried, including 24,000 in one mass grave, and visited later by Hitler in the Nazi occupation of France. The cemetery is worth an entire study, but for purposes here it records the names of 3,000 German schoolboys who died in the First Battle of Ypres. We are familiar with the use of children in the defense of Berlin thirty years later in the desperate, final days of the Third Reich, but at the outset of the Great War the use of children was an established norm. Fifteen percent of all German fighters at the First Battle of Ypres were children, in the face of standing British army professionals. Horace, like Lewis, and so many others on all sides, went to the first industrialized war as a child with the available tools of mass destruction.

Although the details of his rapid transformation from innocent child to scarred adult are largely unknown, the broad brush of Horace's experience resonates with some of larger themes of the War. Horace's child-soldier stature at entry into service speaks to a lost generation of youth, and the logic of stalemate warfare where attrition became the natural means to an end of victory, even if victory were for the last man standing. Horace's role as mounted infantryman speaks to the juxtaposition of contrasting centuries and the clash of industrialization with traditional warfare. And his injuries and final demise speak to a century of weapons of cruelty, mass destruction and the dawn of the era of total war. These warrant some brief contextualizing.

The dusk of horseback warfare that occurred in history at World War I was not a calm sunset but a thunderous cataclysm. We look back aghast at the idea that animal and machinery would be considered compatible, but to the Generals and their training the logic of both was inescapable. Initially, the connection was that which Lewis's service exemplified, namely the use of horse to transport guns. Artillery was deemed essential to break the trench deadlock, and so the horse was as important as the man in this strategy. Depending on the size of the gun, between six and twelve horses were needed to pull it to its staging. Since the numbers of shells involved in the conflict were staggering, there needed to be an almost infinite number of horses used in their delivery. That materiel could only be hauled by truck, man or animal, and animal had, pun excused, the lion's share of the work. The British alone had transported half a million horses to the front lines by 1918, and each week needed to ensure that 34,000 tons of meat and 45,000 tons of bread could be directed to man and horse. And that was just for the artillery, Lewis's home turf.

What of horseback fighting, that Horace was tasked to undertake through his regimental assignmen? Here the beliefs in the supreme advantage of Cavalry attack and the benefits of a mounted infantry ensured the presence of hundreds of thousands of horses in the engagements from the outset, both the British and German armies each moving 100,000 horses to the emerging front in the autumn of 1914. Early propaganda posters by the combatant nations regularly featured horses with soldiers. By the end of the War, only four out of every 100 horses had survived, with a staggering wartime loss total of eight million. Their presence became a major element of wartime experience and strategy, so, for example, the German U-Boat fleet in 1917 had as a primary goal the sinking of all shipping from the United States that contained oats, destined to Europe for the Allied horses. Similarly, the successful British blockade of the German North Sea ports meant that both German civilians and animals were near constant starvation, and the German troops were forced to use saw dust as a food packer for their front line horses. This hellish scenario caused the same symptoms of what is today termed PTSD, then "shell shock," in horse as well as man. Interestingly, troops on all sides noted that the thoroughbred horses suffered most from shell shock, and the ordinary plain farm horse that Lewis and Horace tended were the most competent and durable. *War Horse*—the play by Michael Morpurgo and the movie directed by Steven Spielberg—reinforces that point dramatically.

Of course, the Great War is that conflict most associated with the birth of our awareness of PTSD. Scratchy black and white silent movies have come to us over a century of tortured men, pathetically broken physically and psychologically, and consigned to psychiatric institutions. If there can be any sense of purpose in the destroyed lives and shell shocked minds of the Great War, it is best remembered through the works of the poets of the Great War rather than in any great strides in medical science. Cynically, shell shock was the rationale cited for enforced detention of dissidents in controlled facilities, and in so doing the great legacies of the poets Siegfried Sassoon, Robert Graves, and Wilfred Owen were born, where they shared their detention. That silver lining of the Great War still shines today. The reader is well advised to examine not only the unique body of literature that is First World War poetry, but also works such as the fictional trilogy by Pat Barker,[5] starting with Sassoon's experience in her first book *Regeneration*, about how "shell shock" gave birth to a depth of human insight within tragic conditions, a theme Shakespeare had portrayed earlier in *King Lear*.

For Horace, this trauma was personal. My grandfather, though hospitalized only for physical injury late in the War, thereafter suffered privately and greatly from

[5] Three books: *Regeneration*; *The Eye in the Door*; *The Ghost Road*.

emotional trauma that haunted him for the rest of his life. My mother recounted that her father Horace endured frequent nightmares centered on the same experience for his remaining years of adulthood. Details of his actual historical engagements are lost to history, though it was certain that he was part of the Sherwood Foresters' campaign on the Western Front, and not in the Middle East. He had a very close friend who was also in the mounted infantry, and we know that his friend was a devout Roman Catholic, though sadly we do not know his name. During one assault, side-by-side, a shell blast decapitated Horace's friend, but left Horace himself unscathed. On the field of combat, Horace retrieved from his friend's corpse a small gold pennant of the Virgin Mary. I keep it on my dresser in a box of cufflinks and watches. I suspect that for Horace its significance was a reminder of the Cross as a Christian symbol of suffering and also the spiritual and emotional bond with a loved, mourned comrade.

What is clear is that religion played a role in my grandfather's coping with service on the Western Front, as well as lead a purposeful life thereafter. The phrase "there are no atheists in a foxhole" is well known. The same existential truth has existed throughout human conflict. By the time of the Great War, the participating nations were both technologically and scientifically advanced, and culturally and traditionally religious. The 19th century debates of religion and science had done little to undermine religiosity, and the armies that marched across the planet in World War I were comprised primarily of combatants who believed in God and participated in religious organized community: church, temple, synagogue or mosque. Horace was a primary example of such a believing soldier. He was a man who, despite witnessing vast suffering, held to the sanctity of life, the sacredness of our world, and the beneficence of a loving God. He was an English Christian who exemplified the best of Anglican instincts and held onto them through his life, believing in the strength of Light in the midst of Dark. The fact that his closest friend was a Catholic speaks to an ecumenism that is a very English trait and deeply enriching of religious relations. So I imagine his retrieval of his friend's pennant was significant in sacred as well as personal terms: an act of faith and of love in the midst of a wicked place and time.

The comfort of faith was powerful amidst the fear and horror. It is likely that Horace would have welcomed the Bibles and religious pamphlets that were distributed by the religious societies, especially the Salvation Army. On 25 August 1914, just three weeks after War's start, Lord Robert's of the Naval & Military Bible Society of London and its Scripture Gift Mission issued a pocket-size edition of Saint John's gospel to all British and Empire soldiers. Its front cover instructs the soldier, "Please carry this in your pocket and read it every day." Inside the front cover, Lord Roberts encourages as follows: "I ask you to put your trust in God. He will watch over you and strengthen you. You will find in this little

Book guidance when are you are in health, comfort when you are in sickness, and strength when you are in adversity."[6]

On the last page of the gospel booklet is a letter to the Scripture Gift Mission from an anonymous soldier, noting that having received brought "great consolation," and that: "When at night I have been on duty alone with Him by my side, and the Germans but thirty yards away, I realized that I needed more than my own courage to stand the strain. When the shells of the enemy have burst periodically at my feet I have marveled at the fact of being alive."[7]

This personal response by the fighting soldier to his ever-present mortality was of a different ilk than the official, public references to God that each nation professed. The religiosity of European civilization at the start of the twentieth century also produced a public confidence in the rightness and morality of each nation's cause, and it is one small but dangerous step from a just war conviction to the belief that God is fighting on one's side. Abraham Lincoln's wise rumination that "my concern is not whether God is on our side; my greatest concern is to be on God's side, for God is always right," was largely absent from the officialdom on all sides. Instead, the prevailing mood of "For God and Country" (*Pro Aris*

[6] Scripture Gift Mission (1914): "The Gospel According to St. John—Active Service" (London).

[7] Scripture Gift Mission: "The Gospel According to St. John—Active Service" (London, 1914).

et Focis) was the motto of many British regiments, and similarly the German "Gott Mit Uns" ("God With Us") was standard for all German soldiers, emblazoned on their uniform belt buckle and stylized according to each German state or province. Interestingly, Hitler permitted the Wehrmacht in World War Two to continue using buckles with the same insignia and wording.

There is no information on how Horace viewed this public, nationalist vision of divine preference. The evidence from his post-War life suggests his was a genuine faith and one that sustained him on the battle field, and shaped his commitment thereafter as a faithful Anglican. If he did not use God to justify carnage, neither would it seem did the carnage destroy his faith in God. Nor did he remark openly about the exhortations for or the protests against the War, and their religious justifications, that others like Siegfried Sassoon did in his famous 1917 published letter and in his poem *They*, which satirized the official religious stance on the War: "The Bishop tells us: 'When the boys come back they will not be the same; for they'll have fought In a just cause: they lead the last attack on Anti-Christ'...And the Bishop said: 'The ways of God are strange!'"[8]

In this context of existential trauma and spiritual agony my grandfather was thrown into the breach of the Western Front. From his horse to the trench and onward into no-man's-land, his was the same duty that

[8] Siegfried Sassoon, "They" in *The Old Hunstman and Other Poems* (New York: Holt: 1918).

finally committed ten million around the world to a premature grave and assigned tens of millions more to a life, short or long, of physical and emotional damage. To that latter group Horace was to belong. For when the boys came back, they indeed were not the same.

6.

Gas! Gas! Quick Boys! An Ecstasy of Fumbling

The technology of warfare was harmonized in the advent of weapons of mass destruction in the Great War. Although all combatant nations were researching the most effective way of connecting technology to the delivery of destruction at an industrial level, the Germans are historically marked with its most potent and symbolic form in the use of gas warfare. This is an ironic twist of fate and fortune. The scientist behind the development of gas warfare, initially in its chorine form, was Fritz Haber, sometimes known as the "father of chemical warfare." His research and development expertise in the military use of gases certainly was the major force behind its first major scale use at the Second Battle of Ypres in spring 1915. But the badge of dishonor is unfortunate too, because Haber also dedicated his work in chemistry—and specifically nitrogen and hydrogen—to the development of ammonia-based fertilizers for maximizing crop production. Some estimates put his impact on agriculture as positively impacting food sources for half the world's population in the first half of the twentieth century. Maybe both the labels of evil genius or virtuous godsend simply get it wrong. Haber was a brilliant scientist, whose patriotism put his brilliance at the disposal of German militarism during the War. His brilliance was equally recognized in 1918 at the War's conclusion in his being awarded the Nobel Prize for Chemistry for the invention of the Haber-Bosch Process that would revolutionize agriculture.

In 2015 I visited Langemark German cemetery near Ypres, Belgium. I had visited it several times over the decades, and was this time especially impressed by an outdoor museum that had been established via a grant from the European Union and the United Nations. On the edge of the cemetery and its adjacent fields, the museum had been constructed as a centennial exhibit and memorial to the use of gas warfare in 1915 and the line of attack across twenty kilometers where the gas was used. At the end of the walking museum is a large signpost, pointing to places and dates around the world where gas warfare has been used since its birth on Flanders Fields, including today's horrific civil, multinational, and multi-ethnic conflict in Syria.

The actual birth of gas warfare has a specific date and event. That event also connects directly in warfare experience to another of my relatives, Walter Gower, whom I discuss later. Its birth though is symbolic as powerfully for Horace, who was living his last weeks with chronic lung disease when I sat as a child on his tartan blanket on his lap. Much has been written for decades about the German use of chlorine gas on 22

April 1915 that launched the four-week Second Battle of Ypres, with its 125,000 dead and missing. The bare facts give sufficient factual detail to realize its horrendous nature and implications for a new level of cruelty and inhumanity. When the wind was favorable, blowing east to west, in that spring afternoon the Germans released by hand valve 170 tons of heavy chlorine from 6000 canisters, each weighing about forty kilos along a seven kilometer line of the Ypres salient. The cloud drifted across no-man's-land and caught thousands of French Empire and British Empire troops in bewildered shock. During this and a subsequent gas attack two days later, approximately 8000 troops, primarily Algerian and Canadian, were killed or severely injured, with chlorine acting as an agent on all tissues containing water, thus blinding or drowning the victims in their own lungs. German casualties were also in the hundreds, since the hand release of the gas was poorly executed and in some places the wind turned and blew the cloud of chlorine back into their own trenches.

The German use of gas provoked international condemnation, despite clear evidence that the British and the French were already developing chemical weapons and the French had tried unsuccessfully to use bromide as a weapon at War's start in 1914. The general condemnation though was predictable and evinced on the basis that the Hague Conventions of 1899 and 1907 had already termed chemical weapon usage as a "war crime." The immediate diplomatic spat, in mutual exchanges of accusation of war crimes or hypocrisy, was carried out in the ministries of Paris and Berlin, while the ordinary soldier lived now with the reality of a new threat to face in the conflict.

Early defenses were very crude, with soldiers learning that a urine-soaked rag provided a basic defense, with the ammonia counteracting the chlorine. The rag was held in place by the nick-named "black veil," until in the summer of 1915 a primitive gas mask was released to Allied soldiers, including hood and eye pieces. The British General Douglas Haig had no reservations about chemical use, and in September 1915 the British attack at Loos saw its inaugural Allied use, albeit in a disastrous way for the British when the wind blew the gas back onto the British trenches. The Battle of Loos is interesting in several ways, other than its cost of 100,000 dead in a one month period and failed to alter the course of the War. The battle was the experience that gave Robert Graves the material for his famous post-war memoir, *Goodbye to All That*, and it was also the battle where Queen Elizabeth II's uncle, the older brother of the late Queen Mother, was killed in action. Its use of gas, now also in forms of phosgene and mustard ensured that by the end of 1915 all warring nations had embraced the new, lethal form of total war. Yet it was a method of conflict with patchy results. The invention of a more developed gas mask, captured in thousands of images of men and horses wearing strange elongated nose pieces, made fighting hard. The clumsiness of these devices in conflict was obvious, and ironically the horses often mistook them for oat-bags and would try to eat them, thus rendering them ineffective. Later the use of artillery shells to deliver gas made the deadly chemicals more effective, and hideously difficult to predict. And to make matters even more unpredictable and deadly, the nature of mustard gas was that in cold weather it stuck to clothing in solid form, turning vaporous and lethal when troops wandered into warmer dug-outs, a process ironically known to chemistry as sublimation. To give warning of an attack, wooden rattles were invented that after the War were popularized at British soccer games to cheer on the teams. During the War they were the sound of imminent death.

Wilfred Owen's poem, *Dulce et Decorum Est*, written late 1917 or early 1918 when the Germans had switched solely to the more potent mustard gas, is the literary creation that for a century has most powerfully conveyed the horrors of gas warfare and established it as a symbol for the War itself. One stanza captures the excruciation and suffering of gas warfare:

> Gas! GAS! Quick, boys!—An ecstasy of fumbling
> Fitting the clumsy helmets just in time,
> But someone still was yelling out and stumbling
> And flound'ring like a man in fire or lime.—
> Dim through the misty panes and thick green light,
> As under a green sea, I saw him drowning.
> In all my dreams before my helpless sight,
> He plunges at me, guttering, choking, drowning.

Equally powerful are the images of blinded troops, with rags over their burning eyes, walking in single line with their hand on the shoulder of the man in front, the blind leading the blind in desperate search of respite from the fighting and the horror.

It is this reality that Horace was to confront personally. His military engagements are now lost to history. But family memory suggests that his service was in France with the Sherwood Foresters for the duration of the War until 1917 when he became a victim of a mustard gas attack. It is known that the German use of mustard gas was the preferred method of chemical warfare by 1917. Until that time the Sherwood Foresters were associated with major engagements of the Western Front, notable among them being: Hooge & Sanctuary Wood; the Hohenzollern Redoubt; Vimy Ridge at the Somme; Gommecourt; and Hill 65 & Hill 70. These battles are well documented in military records, and sufficiently represent the stereotype of the water-logged trenches and corpse-strewed wastelands. In 1917 the "Hot Stuff" (mustard gas) as the Tommies termed it was used increasingly by Germans as part of an arsenal to break the deadlock. The test for mustard gas was primarily smell, but that was completely unreliable in terms of environment, especially where temperatures varied, with competing smells of cordite and corpses, and the natural de-sensitization exposure produced.

So Horace, having survived three years of conflict in the mounted infantry, finally succumbed to a non-lethal dose of mustard gas exposure in 1917, and was returned to "Blighty," the old preferred nick-name among troops for Britain, to recuperate. Little is known of his treatment and demobilization. He did not return to the Western Front again during the combat period, so one might assume that his injury was serious enough for an honorable discharge from the army. He thus became one of a million men who were exposed to the horrors of gas during the Great War, but not one of the 100,000 who were killed by its effects. His final year in Flanders was one of extraordinary struggle and innovation by the combatant armies. His role in the mounted infantry would have seen the emergence, albeit in sketchy terms at first, of the new technology of the British "Mark 1" tank, which would eventually lead to the redundancy of the horse in combat. But the two-year emergence of the tank, from its first ineffective launch at the Battle of the Somme in September 1915 to its full effect with 400 vehicles at the Battle of Cambrai in November 1917, was precisely the period when Horace was engaged in a conflict where old and new warfare technologies rode into battle side by side. Indeed, one of the shocking statistics of the new technology is that it failed to provide greater defense in many circumstances. More British tank soldiers died of carbon monoxide poisoning within the tank itself than from enemy fire. Horace's injuries were not sustained because of his increased vulnerability from an outdated technology (of horsepower), but ironically from the very advance in industrialized technology that could produce gas, flamethrower, tank, plane and U-boat. In short, the War saw a complex interplay of old and new in a savage dance of death. The victory parades in the Allied capitals of Europe in 1918 all showcased endless lines of tanks and new technologies before jubilant crowds, but the reality of the conflict was one of disorder, chaos and cruelty, with old and new alike in a frenzy of chance, arbitrariness and destruction, at the whim of the "slings and arrows of fortune." While the tanks were on display for victory, the reality that tank men died of carbon monoxide poisoning from within was overlooked. Such was this Great War.

After the Armistice, I know of two new life-changing events that occurred for Horace. Most importantly, he met Mabel Drywood, closely named but of no relation, and Horace and Mabel married in the early 1920s. If my mother were alive, I would be able to identify the date of their wedding, but that is now lost to history. We rightly understand marriage as a life changing event. After experiencing at first hand the Great War, it might seem trite to describe marriage as life changing in any sense. A global cataclysm that took 10 million lives and wounded another 25 million is surely the central event of significance to those who were part of that story. But I consider Horace might, like his comrades, have viewed that the ordinariness of life is as important and meaningful to the returning veterans as the trauma of global conflict and its impact on us. Indeed, the lost generation of Flanders and continents beyond would likely have estimated that their ultimate sacrifice was indeed to protect that ordinariness. It was not only a struggle of nations, but moreover a struggle of the right to be, to live, to do good, to make mistakes, to procreate, to grow old quietly and to die in as ordinary a way as possible in our own private, and family lives. So Horace exemplified an ordinary life after an extraordinary youth, he married Mabel, and built a new life as an ordinary man and citizen.

The ghosts of Flanders were surely close to him and to Mabel, though. For, another life-changing event of genealogical importance was something that Horace chose to undertake. In itself it was a small act in the play of his life, but it was symbolically extraordinary and has grown over the century of its happening into something of significance to my family. This illustrates why genealogy and the War is something of an ongoing story that has importance in our lives. The next section of this book will focus on another family member who did not return from the War of 1914–18, Private Walter Gower, of the four-hundred year old infantry regiment of the "Buffs" of east Kent. Walter was Mabel's much loved older Uncle and his death in the War caused Mabel, my grandmother, much grief. Either during their betrothal or when newly-weds, Mabel sorely wished someone to locate the final resting place of her Uncle Walter, and to leave a memorial at his gravesite. So, out of love for his new wife Horace returned—when his health allowed—to the killing fields of Flanders, an act of courage and devotion. Most veterans never chose to return to the land where such suffering had been endured. The poem by Rupert Brooke, *The Soldier*, had already gained notoriety during the War, not least due to Brooke's death in 1915 in combat, and it reads as a romanticized grieving to those who fell and of the inherent rightness of the cause. One line poignantly and notably summed up the connection already emerging during the War between Flanders and memorialized grief:

> *If I should die, think only this of me:*
> *That there's some corner of a foreign field that is*
> *forever England.*

The corner of that foreign field was the place where the loved uncle of Horace's bride now lay buried under a wooden cross at that time, and Horace was returning alone to the scarred, former war zone to pay personal and family respects on behalf of his wife. This visit occurred a few years after the War and about the same time as the great memorials and rituals associated with the Armistice began to emerge in the 1920s. Walter Gower's record in the official Graves Registration Report is dated to January 1921, with the detail that a personalized wooden cross was erected. It is therefore safe to assume that Horace made his journey after that record was established. It was a personal pilgrimage that surely was taken at much emotional cost, and yet became unwittingly an act of familial legacy that speaks to us today.

His life at home gave him that second chance at ordinariness. Horace and Mabel Wood lived in suburban London, gave birth to two children, Ken and Patricia (Paddy), my mother, and he was successful as a businessman working for an American corporation, Standard Electric. He was so promising as a young employee of the corporation that he was offered a management role in Australia for a primary project in the building of the Sydney Harbor Bridge, construction of which began in July of 1923. Whether out of love for his new wife, or concern about his own health, he chose to stay with Standard Electric in London, and was successful there too. During the 1930s, when the Great Depression hit, he elected to take a one-third cut in salary like his employees, in order to keep people in work. My father met my mother in their teens, became sweet-hearts, maintained their relationship during my father's absence overseas in the Royal Navy, and they married in 1949. Both Horace and Lewis were in attendance with their wives Lydia and Mabel, and thus the old soldiers of the Great War were able to see the next generation grow together. He was, according to several sources, a compassionate, inquisitive, conversational, and joyful man, who enjoyed politics and philosophy.

And we also know that his bond with his comrades existed at two enduring levels. My mother had a medal that was given to the winning team of a local 1924 amateur football (soccer) tournament, in which, despite his lung injuries, Horace played. The team was comprised of

Veterans from all services in the Raynes Park area of London, termed the London Rifles but comprised of a rag tag group of men of the Great War. Whereas the initial rush to war had tragically maintained local town associations in the regiments, thus decimating entire communities when the battle casualties were so high, this time the local comrades could enjoy life and association together at a time now of peace. And surely the symbolism was not lost of them of the defiant and beautiful Christmas truce of 1914, when famously British and Saxon troops played a game of soccer in no-man's-land and exchanged stories, food and drink, after hearing the singing of *Silent Night* from each other's trenches. The soccer ball was also tragically a symbol of the first day of the Somme, when at least two were kicked across no-man's-land during the mass slaughter, one ascribed thus: "the great European Cup-Tie Final: East Surreys v Bavarians. Kick off at Zero."[1] The memory of such would surely not have been lost on Horace and his team comrades as they redeemed the game in the 1920s.

Secondly, when Britain found itself a generation later at war again with Nazi Germany, Horace offered his service as a recruit to Britain's Home Guard, the reserve service comprised primarily of Great War veterans, as a member of the 53rd (Surrey) Battalion. The guard provided part-time service in territorial Britain, primarily tasked with support to usual military units in the event of a German land invasion. Since that never occurred,

[1] Sheffield, *The First World War in 100 Objects,* 140.

the Home Guard was used typically for air raid duty, fire-fighting support, and other emergency management of the civilian population. His experience landed him the role of Commander in his local Kingston unit, showing that whatever the difficult experiences of the Great War, he was willing to serve his homeland a generation later in the titanic struggle against totalitarianism that was World War II.

I consider myself very fortunate to have that single memory of my grandfather, Horace, at the start of my life and the close of his, of sharing a moment in time and space, me sitting with my kindly ill grandfather, who seems less old now as I age. The epitaph is true for Horace. Age did not weary him, nor the years condemn, even if it was inscribed originally in honor of those who never returned. Instead Horace held steady, and paid it forward, as the saying goes, with a life of purpose and commitment to a common good, even when his early life had turned violent, ugly and demonic. For Horace, in that darkness, there was a light that would be followed back from the fields of Flanders and onward for the remainder of his days. Today, my family is still enlightened by his life's legacy.

AN EYE FOR AN EYE: ALLIED GAS ATTACK

French soldiers making a gas and flame attack on German trenches in Flanders on 1 January, 1917. After the initial launch of gas warfare in the spring of 1915 by the Germans, both Allied and Central Powers forces adopted the use of chemical warfare.

7.

Then it's Tommy This, an' Tommy That, an' Tommy How's Yer Soul?

Families by nature intersect the lives of their individual members in and through time. For my two grandfathers that intersection between them occurred in the decades following the War, with the courtship and eventual wedding of my parents, Peter and Patricia (or Paddy). It would be interesting to surmise that these two old soldiers whose children joined a new family branch might have engaged in private conversations about their war experiences.

But my third family member in this genealogy has a more poignant connection to family intersections, even posthumously. Private Walter Gower, as mentioned earlier, was the young and loved uncle of Horace's new bride, and his wartime death prompted Horace to make that post-War family pilgrimage on behalf of Mabel. It is very hard to know the emotional toll this act took. Many soldiers never returned understandably to the combat zones they had inhabited. The trauma for many was too great ever to permit any spatial proximity. The great memorialization process across the continents—both at home and abroad at the distant sites of battles fought—only began in the early 1920s, four years or so after the end of hostilities, reflecting a societal grieving process that like individuals took years to experience. Adam Hochschild's outstanding book, *To End All Wars,*[1] notes that in 1920 Britain marked the second anniversary of Armistice Day, and the burial of Britain's Unknown Warrior at Westminster Abbey, with two minutes of silence at the 11th hour when it had come into effect. No-one predicted the same experience across the country that every newspaper recorded of those two minutes: complete silence and lack of activity at work, in public and at home, except for the sound of sobbing women everywhere.

It is clear that my grandmother's grief for her dead Uncle motivated my grandfather's brave return to the fields of Flanders. His own trauma and grieving for his lost comrades were also doubtless real. His courage prevailed and that he was able to locate and pay respect at the gravesite of Private Walter Gower. At that time, and until the Commonwealth Graves Commission established the famous and simple Portland headstones in the 1920s that adorn military cemeteries and are now showing decades of weathering, the war dead were signified with a wooden cross, bearing the name and rank of the deceased, and date of death if known on the registry. Thus Horace and Walter at some unknown time but at a specific place in both space and time found their histo-

[1] Adam Hochschild, *To End all Wars: A Story of Loyalty and Rebellion* (New York: Houghton-Mifflin, 2011) 34-38.

ries and memories intersecting across death's finality in an unkempt cemetery in a desperate, war-ravaged place in Flanders. Clearly Horace's journey became an esteemed family story, that my grandmother and mother proudly remembered, with the tinge of sadness that the location of Walter's grave was only ever known to Horace. His passing in the 1960s had removed any possibility of further respect or visit to the resting place of a dead war soldier and former family member. For eighty-five years the grave of Walter Gower remained unknown and unvisited by my family aside from Horace's original, vicarious pilgrimage.

Then, in 1995, I discovered transformational data, namely that Britain's Commonwealth War Graves Commission had achieved the extraordinary feat of publishing on its website the known basic data of all dead of Britain and its Empire from the 20th Century wars. In one afternoon of web searching through the research engine of the CWGC the decades of uncertainty was replaced by clear and immediate information on Walter's burial location. His resting place was listed in an official record, with accompanying certificate of remembrance, in a communal cemetery in Bailleul, France near to a psychiatric hospital that had acted as a major field hospital of the Ypres salient. That communal cemetery contained the allied dead of two wars as well as the local citizens of the town, perhaps reflecting that all are equal in death. Walter's death at the age of twenty-three occurred on 25 April 1915, and his full regimental details were clearly recorded. As a participant in several tours of the Western Front I begin piecing a family puzzle together, and the picture was a new one that injected added pathos and pride into the life and death of my Great, Great Uncle Walter.

The date of late April 1915 and the location of the Ypres Salient is a period of infamy in military history, as noted earlier. The debasing of human conflict that had occurred there three days prior to Walter's death was the baptism of chemical warfare in the chlorine gas attack of 22 April. Both the Allied and Central powers had been acutely aware that the stalemate along the Western Front could only be broken by the invention of edge weaponry that exceeded the technological prowess of the opposing side decisively, if a desperate war of attrition was to be circumvented. The mass production of airplanes, machine gun, flamethrower, and shrapnel shell were examples of the belief in technological ingenuity would grant the winning edge.

The effects were immediate and devastating, routing the Allies so quickly that the Germans were surprised and ill-prepared for a strategic follow up. The 8,000 casualties that fell over the next forty-eight hours were the first of a cohort that numbered more than 90,000 deaths by gas by 1918. On the first night of that 22 April attack, those Germans that did move forward often found themselves stumbling into their own deadly chlorine gas in deserted trenches. The effect of the gas was overwhelming on the thousands of individual soldiers—causing drowning within the lungs through the burning of organs—and temporarily reshaping the entire Front itself. The new technology had indeed achieved overwhelming effective surprise, punching a six kilometer hole into the impregnable Western Front and leaving a gap that if capitalized upon would enable a rapid movement on Paris and a quick victory for the Central Powers.

Corporal Anthony R. Hossack of the Queen Victoria Rifles was deployed there that fateful day and recorded his observations for posterity:

> Plainly something terrible was happening. What was it? Officers, and Staff officers too, stood gazing at the scene, awestruck and dumbfounded; for in the northerly breeze there came a pungent nauseating smell that tickled the throat and made our eyes smart. The horses and men were still pouring down the road, two or three men on a horse, I saw, while over the fields streamed mobs of infantry, the dusky warriors of French Africa. .. One man came stumbling through our lines. An officer of ours held him up with levelled revolver, "What's the matter, you bloody lot of cowards?" says he. The Zouave was frothing at the mouth, his eyes started from their sockets, and he fell writhing at the officer's feet. "Fall in!" Ah! We expected that cry.[2]

My first visit to Walter's grave earlier in 2007 had clearly suggested that he too had been a victim of this

---

[2] Lewis, *A Brief History of World War I*, 90.

German gas attack. His grave is located in a shared military and civilian cemetery in the heart of Bailleul, and he is buried in a single grave with another victim according to the headstone. His death, two days after the gas attack, suggested a grim demise over forty-eight hours, with the large sanatorium acting as the field hospital for his final hours. This sobering notion seemed persuasive, and provided our family a sense of closure on his final circumstances. For years I assumed its veracity until the spring 2015. At that time, when revisiting his gravesite to commemorate the centennial anniversary day of his passing, two problems emerged to the "gas victim" hypothesis that were brought to light with research jointly undertaken with a local historian and guide, Koenraad Dumoulin.

Firstly, in re-visiting his grave I learned that the 8,000 victims of the German gas attack were not recovered from the battlefield nor made their way to the Bailleul field hospital until several days after the attack. The fact that his corpse was identified, marked and deposited in a two-person grave on 25 April was testimony both to his spending time in the sanatorium field hospital and that his grave today was the same as the day he was buried, in short that there was no exhumation and re-burial prior to his final resting place. Moreover, the date of his death was too soon after the 22 April gas assault to allow him to be removed from the battlefield, hospitalized and then buried. In short, his death was now likely to be as coincidental with, rather than instrumental of, the German gas attack. A second more compelling piece of evidence also emerged to challenge the gas victim hypothesis. On closer look, it seemed odd that an infantryman of the Buffs 2nd Battalion East Kent regiment would be alongside Canadian and French lines in that sector of the Salient. What does emerge importantly, however, is that the Buffs did take part in later action that was a result of the German gas assault, and that this subsequent role can be seen as one of the most significant of the Great War, at a time when the Allied lines had collapsed after the German attack. Historians call that action the Geddes Detachment, and my Great, Great Uncle indeed did have a line in the play that was this particular piece of war theatre.

After the Germans had opened a six-kilometer gap north of Ypres on the evening of 22 April, the Western Front was exposed and vulnerable in the extreme. Two battalions, one being the 2nd Buffs, and a second division of cavalry were ordered into a stop formation at the crossroads in the center of the village of St Jean, where thousands of French and colonial French troops had retreated in panic at the clouds of gas blowing eastward. During the night various battalions and regiments in the region were rushed into the same area under the command of Colonel A.D. Geddes of the Buffs. Meanwhile the Canadians were in dire predicament defending St. Julien Wood, with thousands of them already casualties of the gas. At this point the Allied armies were in disarray and despairing. Had the Germans anticipated the effectiveness of their new chemical weapon, the road to Ypres and onto Paris would be open. That night and early next morning Colonel Geddes managed to position his rag-tag division of seven aggregated battalions into critical positions at St. Jean and St. Julien Wood. The inevitable German advance failed to materialize, with German records indicating that no consideration of reserves had been built into the Gas plan, and that most German troops did not have effective masks to proceed. Indeed, hundreds of Germans stumbled onward into their own deadly clouds of poison during the night, suffering the same outcome.

By morning the crossroads at St. Jean was still in the hands of the English Buffs, and young Private Walter Gower was to face his last action and his last day alive. When two additional battalions arrived, they joined with the beleaguered Canadians at St. Julien Wood, providing a cobbled random line of resistance. Geddes will be remembered to history as a courageous officer whose ingenuity and risk saved the collapse of the Ypres salient and whose command orders brought grief into my family. That noon Geddes, still bewildered by the absence of a proper German assault after the opening of the Front the night before, ordered a counterattack toward the abandoned Front Line. The battlefield at St. Jean is well preserved, showing the furious nature of the Allied counterattack. That day the Germans were stemmed, and the battle raged on until its zenith on 8 May. Walter Gower never survived the first day of the counterattack, an action now subsumed under the larger and notorious name of the Second Battle of Ypres. On the first day he was in some unknown fashion mortally wounded and taken to the enormous Casualty Clearing Station that is now the sprawling Psychiatric Hospital of Bailleul, where he died of his wounds two days later. The long assumed belief that he was a victim of the infamous Gas attack was laid to rest as a plausible but erroneous conclusion. His body and others at the clearing station were then identified and buried in the local Bailleul cemetery, where lack of space meant that bodies were regularly stacked three to a grave. His gravesite was then marked with a wooden cross at the time, and remains in its same original location today, now with a replacement Portland headstone that the Commonwealth War Commission gave to each victim in the 1920s. Walter had died on the first day of the Second Battle of Ypres, as part of the Geddes Detachment's frantic but successful efforts to prevent the collapse of the Western Front in the Ypres Salient after the first use of chemical weapons in any organized way in the history of human conflict.

One hundred years to the day of his sacrifice, in April 2015, members of my immediate family and I visited his grave, conducted a brief religious service and planted at his gravesite a red poppy—the universal symbol of the lost generation of the First World War. My twenty-three-year old Great, Great Uncle Walter was given his funeral rites exactly 100 after he gave his life to help prevent the Kaiser's army from reaching the gates of Paris and ensuring the victory of German militarism in the spring 1915.

8.

THEIR NAME LIVETH FOR EVERMORE

The pathos of my Great, Great Uncle's death was a single example of a vast story of loss a century ago. The very first and very last British victims of the War are strangely buried, without any prior planning, just three grave sites apart from each other. While only three names lie between these bookends of four years and four months of carnage, another one million names of British and Empire dead could have been placed between them. By the time the Armistice came into effect on the 11th hour of the 11th day of the 11th month, ten million young men had vanished into the earth, into silence and into history. An additional seven million civilians were killed in the Great War, and an additional twenty-five million veterans were injured for the rest of their lives, including Horace Holbrook and his damaged lungs. The "War to End All Wars" had changed human existence forever with a cascade of death unseen in all of humankind's 85,000 years of life on this planet. Absurdly, to the insult of man-made annihilation in those four years was added the injury of natural disease, when another ten million were to die in the next twelve months of Spanish influenza. The scale of death and suffering produced by the Great War was almost as hard to comprehend as the scale of the distance between the visible stars we observe in the night sky. After the Armistice, signed at 5:00 A.M. on 11 November another six hours elapsed before the formal cessation of hostilities at 11:00 A.M., and the then issuance of the eponymous telegram from the German Front Line to Berlin HQ, "All Quiet on the Western Front." During those six hours from the ink drying on the agreement to the quiet sacredness of the larks singing high above the silent trenches, new warring ferocity occurred, now including American troops. In those six final hours, a further 3,000 Allied died in combat along the Front. It is of little surprise that the sounds of weeping were the only sounds that disturbed the mournful silence that was annually memorialized on Armistice Day in the 1920s.

Walter is memorialized not only in the communal cemetery in Bailleul, France, but also back in his home town. The ancient Kentish Buffs have fought and died for nearly five centuries on the fields of Europe from Reformation times. Though their roots spring from the soil of Kent, "the garden of England," with its historic oast houses (breweries), windmills and famed chalked cliffs of Dover, towering high and leaning toward continental Europe. Chaucer's Canterbury Tales had conveyed the ancient Albion that the county of Kent embodies, and Chaucer's use of term "weald" or wild and untamed countryside, is still is a popular description of Kent's beauty, understood today more as a garden sanctuary than a wild place. In this ancient county its parish churches were built from the time of Plantagenet kings, and Walter's home village of Cranbrook is the place of St. Dunstan's Parish Church, built in the fifteenth century. Locally it is known romantically and unofficially as "the Cathedral of the Weald." Inside St. Dunstan's is an engraved stone plaque, typical of many English churches, that records the names of the 107 men from the village who died in the Great War. Another plaque in the church records separately the names of the twenty-five villagers who died in World War Two. The plaque dedicated to the fallen of the Great War is dedicated "to the memory of the men of Cranbrook who fell in the Great War 1914–1918. Greater Love Hath No Man Than This." The name "Gower W" is inscribed toward the bottom of the left-hand panel. The listing of the dead with their surname listed ahead of their first name echoes the formality of Britain's education system, where all pupils were once addressed by their family surname.

My parents visited the church after the re-discovery of his French grave and paid further family homage to a young man who did not live long nor know his future genealogy, but has since claimed an honored place in the memory of family generations. My parents' visit was marred by the unwelcome occurrence of the theft of my mother's purse that day, thus reinserting abruptly the randomness and unpredictability of the present into treasured moments of past reflections. If their church visit was spoiled because of an unfortunate and random act of theft, I suspect that would not have surprised or disturbed Private Walter Gower or any of his comrades. For them life was to be lived in the moment, with sacred moments shared ephemerally and ripped apart arbitrarily between and among allies. For those sanctified moments would indeed be taken suddenly away with little logic, justice, explanation or timeliness. The hallowed moments of love would be fleeting, even if a century later they would be honored.

How that reality played out in the lives of Walter's parents has no record. My grandmother Mabel alone brought us the story of Walter's short life and early death alongside the millions of his generation. The Commonwealth War Graves Commission website[1] provides Walter, and all its recorded dead, a standardized certificate that is "commemorated in perpetuity" and features a large photo of the base of the Whitehall Cenotaph, the most famous memorial to the Great War in the world, adorned with two poppy wreaths and the final statement of remembrance in Britain, "Their Name Liveth for Evermore." The particulars of Walter's military service and genealogical context are contained in two sentences at the top of the certificate. The first records his regimental number (L/8625) in the Second Battalion of the Buffs and his date of death and age at his death, on that late April spring day. Below, the life and genealogy of Walter sits starkly juxtaposed: "Son of George Arthur and Annie Gower, of 1, Horse Entry, High St., Cranbrook, Kent."

---

[1] http://www.cwgc.org/.

Like so many parents my Great, Great, Great Uncle George and Aunt Annie would have grieved deeply at the loss of their only son, Walter. I have thankfully never known the agony of losing a child, the most nightmarish of fears to all loving parents. The great German sculptures of Kathe Kollwitz, whose son Peter shared the same fate in the same place at Walter, portrays the agony of the Grieving Parents (*Die trauernden Eltern*), as her self-statues overlook Peter's grave at Vladslo Cemetery, a few miles from Walter's resting place. No words can express the raw human emotion, the simple monumental grief and guilt of the older generation captured in their statues of the bereaved parents, who helplessly watched their children die in millions for a national cause of utter irrelevance but of absolute tragic threat to the intimacy of parent and child. Ironically, that loss and grief united Kathe Kollwitz with George and Annie, who shared across the killing fields, across national agendas, and across their warring causes a greater bond than most of us will fortunately ever know.

We do know that in the same way that Walter's life is honored in a standard certificate on the website of the Commonwealth War Graves Commission, one hundred years ago his parents George and Annie would have also received a standard notification of his death. For enlisted men that would have been Army Form B104-82, characteristic of a British bureaucracy and efficiency that had built and organized an Empire. The General Post Office was the means of delivery and the terse short notification that George and Annie received would simply have conveyed "deeply regret inform you L/8685, 2nd Bn., Pte. Walter Gower officially reported killed in action 25 April 1915." The effect of receipt of these telegrams (for officers) and Army Forms (for enlisted soldiers) was of course individually devastating, and the material of much legend thereafter, such as that documented by the famous writer Vera Brittain, who received four such notifications. What was especially hard for those immediate kin was the absence of real information, and the knowledge that there would be no repatriation of the body, which was forbidden. In the early War years, when enlistment was accompanied with the motivational promise that friends and families could fight together, the effect of a whole village receiving the same day multiple notifications of death was simply catastrophic. The famous example of the "Salford Pals" regiment is known a century later, but there were many initial battalions that were promptly re-assigned when hundreds of notices of death were delivered simultaneously to the same villages and towns.

Walter Gower's parents would doubtless learn eventually of the whereabouts of his remains, but no family knowledge exists of any visit by them. Horace alone appears to have undertaken that task. Even harder would have been when next of kin learned that no corpse or burial place or marked grave would be possible for their loved one. The Great War produced such levels of destruction that millions of men simply disappeared into explosive fragments or literally sank into the mud. On one visit in 1984 to the Front I discovered inside an old bunker in a farmer's field the skeletal remains and uniform fragments of a victim sticking out of the ground. Two enormous British memorials that I have visited reinforce this point of the missing dead. The Menin Gate or Ypres Memorial, reminiscent of London's Marble Arch and Paris's Arc de Triomphe, hosts nightly at 8:00 P.M. a Last Post bugle ceremony inside its echoing arches, held every day since 1924 except for the period of Nazi occupation of France. The ceremonial bugling is led by a particular regiment that fought in the War and is typically attended by hundreds of tourists, visitors, and European school and college students, moved to solemn silence. The Menin Gate Ypres Memorial lists the names of 54,000 missing British and Empire troops who disappeared in the Ypres Salient. The Salient had a radius of about five kilometers, so the scale of vanishing absence is mind-boggling, particularly when that number excludes the dead and missing of France, Germany and other nations who fought at Ypres. As overwhelming is Sir Edwin Lutyen's Thiepval Monument to the Missing of the Somme, similarly recording the 73,000 British Empire missing from the Battle of the Somme, including Charles Dickens's grandson. The monument's size is hard to comprehend when walking its steps and arches, and the endless list of names everywhere speaks to a conflict of unfathomable description and price. The lack of a burial place was an especially cruel outcome for hundreds of thousands of next of kin to the fallen. The great British poet Rudyard Kipling, whose attitude changed from patriotic jingoism to tragic grief, never accepted the missing-in-action status of his son John who evaporated into history at the Battle of Loos in 1915. For years afterward, Kipling vainly kept visiting and corresponding with leads in Germany in the forlorn hope that his son had become a prisoner-of-war, and was simply needing to be identified.

Arthur and Annie Gower were spared that desperation at least. They could take the crumb of comfort that families around Europe and the world begged for, namely that their boy had a proper resting place and the honor of a hallowed plot that was his earned and saluted piece of a foreign field forever. Why we yearn for this with our dead speaks to the mystery of love, life, and memory. To the fallen, an unknown grave in the mud or at sea or in a shell-blast was no different an outcome than Walter having a marked grave in Bailleul. But for us who remain, we are transfixed and terrorized by the thought that our identity could be so ephemeral and fleeting that we could literally disappear into the universe, as though we had never even existed in the first place outside of time and place, and without heart and soul.

Since 2014 the combatant nations of Europe have been marking the centennial of the War. I have received two related gifts from my sister. One is a ceramic handmade poppy, one of a million that adorned the moat around the Tower of London and that Queen Elizabeth

II attended to commemorate the centennial outbreak of War in August 2014. Each was uniquely handmade to honor the individual million lives that the British Empire gave up for the War to End All Wars. The funds raised go to the care and hospitalization of veterans, through the British Legion. The other gift, in commemoration of the Somme, is a small metal poppy shape, made from shell casings that were retrieved from the Somme battlefield, and that the Somme 100 organization is providing to honor one soldier who fell at one of the costliest events in human history. My poppy is dedicated to Private Luther Creek. He was an infantryman of the West Yorkshire Regiment (Prince of Wales's Own) and died on the 7th day of the 7th month of 1916, just one week into the four-month battle. He is buried, according to the commemorative certificate the Somme 100 program issued with the poppy pin, at the Abbeville Communal Cemetery. He marched and died and is buried in the same fields where Lewis Blake dragged his horse and gun, but unlike Lewis, he did not come home.

As we saw, all British Commonwealth Remembrance memorials were engraved at their base with the phrase, "Their Name Liveth Evermore," taken from the Ecclesiasticus (deuterocanonical Book of Sirach, 44:14) The implications appear clear from the vantage point of history. Whereas the British machinery of war had given rise to the perception of mass death, with little sense of individual worth, and whereas the postal service notification of death was similarly clinical without deference to the uniqueness of the lost lives, here was a memorial phrase attempting something else. It would offer instead an expression of mourning and spirituality, where the name—since so many only had a name and no physical relic to mourn—would be cast into a transcendent context of eternal living. In a sense, it was beautifully fitting for a world now coming to stark terms with the horror and mourning that was globally shared, but uniquely personal to each family, such as that belonging to Arthur and Annie Gower.

Today's Somme 100 remembrance program speaks to a world distanced by history from the Great War and seeks to reinforce why remembrance still matters, if for different reasons. The phrase on the certificate is not the same that Kipling and Lutyens determined was the right one for the grieving world of the lost generation a century ago. The phrase that was chosen now to memorialize the Somme's fallen, including Private Luther Creek, reads: "Every Man Remembered." It is a man, not a name, who died on the Somme: or on Flanders Fields, on or the Gallipoli Peninsula, or in the frozen Carpathians, or on the Atlantic Waters, or in Africa's colonies. And in our world where individual identity counts so much for who we are, the nations of Europe are producing unique non-identical ceramic poppies, or hand-made poppy pins from Somme shell casings, because a living person went and fought and died or came home and their individual life and their individual family histories were changed totally. And it is up to us, today, to remember them: as people whose identities were both individual and collective. The mourning parents of the ten million dead, like Arthur and Annie Gower, did not need to remember. They could not move away from their loss and grief, even if they wanted to. But to us a hundred years later, we would be well advised to remember if we are to know sufficiently who we are and why we are who we are. In remembering we give honor to the grieving generation of Gower, Lutyens, Kipling and their hope that every man and his name does indeed "liveth for evermore," and in doing so gives greater context to our own lives. Walter Gower, Luther Creek, and the ten million fallen would have understood their lives and their deaths to mean something in a particular time and space, and that it all ended on a bloodied field somewhere long disappeared. We have the opportunity and responsibility to do more: to remember, and thereby acknowledge, that their lives continued resonating in the generations that followed and in the families that remembered and mourned their passing, even after their own life's stories were concluded so abruptly and cruelly.

9.

RETREAT, HELL! WE JUST GOT HERE

The title of this chapter repeats the exact exclamation, now well known and proudly recounted by the U.S. Marines, of a certain Capt. Lloyd W. Williams, who commanded the 51st Company of the 2nd Battalion of the 5th Marine Regiment at Belleau Wood. Upon arrival on 2 June 1918 with his company he was informed by a French officer he should immediately retreat his soldiers in the face of a full German assault. His famous response is testimony to the daring courage of the American Doughboys. Williams himself was to die nine days later of gas and shrapnel wounds incurred in battle at Belleau Wood. What circumstances could lead to Capt. Williams's name becoming eponymous for a century of U.S. Marine bravery and American willingness to put its young in harm's way for the good of others?

Despite its best efforts to remain neutral and outside of what was seen by most Americans as a catastrophic European regional conflict, President Woodrow Wilson eventually determined that the nation had no option but to join the Allied effort after nearly three years of determined but painful neutrality. On 6 April 1917 the President received Congress's support for his 2 April request for a declaration of War on Germany, and with the entrance of the United States the Great War was now truly transformed in the First World War. A similar but later US declaration of war against the Central Power of Austro-Hungary occurred belatedly and oddly eight months later in December 1917.

Wilson had been narrowly re-elected as President the preceding November 1916 on the election slogan, "he kept us out of the war." He had indeed succeeded in maintaining American distance from the conflict despite common sympathies for the Allied cause and increasing exasperation with the German war methodology and its deadly impact on Americans. Many Americans had illegally chosen to join the Allied cause, often by crossing into Canada to enlist in the British forces. Perhaps most famously though was the Lafayette Flying Squadron of some 209 early American aviators who had their own squadron within the French Lafayette Escadrille flying corps, from as early as 1915.

The road to War for the United States is beyond this book's focus, but two events of huge significance should be briefly noted as milestones to American entanglement. The first is the sinking of the Lusitania in May 1915, a story the reader is advised to explore in Erik Larsen's brilliant book *Dead Wake*.[1] The Lusitania was such a symbolic crossing of the Rubicon that historians have debated why it alone did not prompt an American declaration. Less mesmerizing but more important

---

[1] Erik Larson, *Dead Wake: The Last Crossing of the Lusitania* (New York: Penguin Random House, 2015).

than the details of the sinking, with its 130 Americans among the total 1,200 perished, is the political and military context, which partly accounts for American reticence to jump into the War after the ship was sunk on 7 May a few miles off the Irish coast. Germany had finally and dramatically determined in February 1915, after fierce internal disagreement between Kaiser, Chancellor and the German High Command, to begin a policy of unrestricted submarine warfare, in an attempt to force the British Grand Fleet back out to the North Sea and Atlantic Ocean and end the blockade of ports along the Belgian, Dutch and German coastlines that could provide food and materiel to Germany. That blockade was proving extraordinarily successful in starving the German people and the German war machine, and Germany knew that unless the Grand Fleet could be forced into deep and distant waters, its war plans were doomed to eventual failure. In that context, the unrestricted submarine policy that deemed any vessel not flying Central Power flags around the British Isles as qualified for sinking without warning seems less cruel. Indeed, German concern and sensitivity to potential accusations of war crimes meant that public relations were ramped up to warn, explain and publicize the new policy to avert those very accusations. On 22 April Germany published full page advertisements in American newspapers, including the New York Times, explaining its policy of unrestricted submarine warfare, and printed a series of warnings to Americans not to sail on the Lusitania. The fact that the ship even sailed seems extraordinary given the benefit of hindsight, but in 1915 the German threat was relegated in importance and American confidence in British high seas control was over-exaggerated. But with its sinking the hard reality of the pain of war hit home to a nation desperate to keep the War over in Europe, even if occasional ignominy and loss of life had to be endured.

The tipping point for America though was the German attempt to stir up conflict between the US and Mexico, in the logical but disastrous assumption that a US-Mexican War would keep Woodrow Wilson and the nation's attention focused solely on its southern border, and not worry about what was happening across the Atlantic. By 1917 war on two fronts was proving too costly for Germany. While dissent in Russia, and the eventual Bolshevik revolution, offered Germany the alluring hope of a peace treaty with Russia, which it did conclude finally in March 1918, Germany knew that it could not sustain prolonged war on both fronts. An early cessation to war on one front was essential, particularly given the stranglehold of the British blockade. While German diplomatic efforts with Russia gained new urgency after the February and October Revolutions in Moscow and St. Petersburg respectively, German strategy posited that a final push in the West was essential ahead of any potential future American involvement. If the American Doughboys even arrived on the Western Front, that front would be lost to the Allies, the thinking went. The Doughboys, a historic term that gained popular usage in the First World War in reference to American troops, were not yet in Flanders. If they could forever be kept away from the Western theatre, then Germany could in theory make a final push on Paris and thus secure victory, once the eastern front was pacified and its troops there transported westward. If the Doughboys were in France though, with huge quantities of men and materiel, that possibility would evaporate. So German priority was on ensuring the US did not enter the War, but instead of using the carrot of diplomacy to entice Wilson to stay away, the Germans foolishly chose the stick of Mexico.

Tensions between the US and Mexico had been strained for some years after the start of the Mexican revolution. By the mid years of the decade they were severe. General John Pershing—later of global fame as the tireless and solitary leader of the American Expeditionary Force in Flanders after the US entry into the War—had pursued the Mexican revolutionary Francisco "Pancho" Villa and his forces inside the Mexican border earlier that year in the Punitive Expedition. Germany sensed in this escalating tension an opportunity to capitalize on a worsening situation on the North American continent, which now saw increasing numbers of federal troops sent to the Texas and Arizona borders with Mexico to suppress any uprising or quell any future conflict. Germany's decision to act and its particular choice of action in this opportunistic context was a colossal mistake, backfiring in spectacular and catastrophic terms.

The Zimmerman Telegram is well known in history. Intriguingly, the Ems Telegram or Ems Dispatch forty seven years earlier in 1870 had triggered a war between Prussia and France that produced magnificent success, unification and strength for Germany. The Zimmerman Telegram of January 1917 conversely can be seen as instrumental to the undoing and devastation of Germany in the Great War. In that month British and American intelligence both intercepted a coded cable from the German Foreign Minister Arthur Zimmerman to his staff in the German Embassy in Mexico City. Ambassador von Eckhardt was instructed to promise Mexico the support of Germany for regaining earlier lost territories in New Mexico, Texas and Arizona, in return for a Mexican invasion of the United States that would, so German logic went, prevent the United States from any military intervention in Europe. The gleeful British decoded the message and presented it in full to the State Department and to the White House in late February. When confronted with its contents by the US in early March, Zimmerman honorably but imprudently admitted completely to its authenticity and origin. To add to the backfire, the reality was that Mexico would never have contemplated full war with its northern neighbor, recognizing its own internal post-revolutionary weakness and fissures. The Zimmerman Telegram pushed Wilson and Congress over the precipice. What the U-Boat campaign and Allied sympathies had been unable to produce was now finally realized with American entrance into World War I due to the public exposure of ill-thought, desperate, and distracting geo-politics that Germany pursued, to its final detriment. In April 1917 the US moved from being the economic engine and supplier of War materials to the combatant nations, which had launched American military-industrial might, to now being a protagonist and participant in the world's greatest military struggle in history.

America's entrance transformed not just national policy and priority, but more existentially the families and individuals whose lives were about to be changed forever, including the seventy-nine men whose names are inscribed on the Coleman Hill Memorial in Macon, Georgia. The winter afternoon when I first encountered the neglected Memorial heralded for me a new, third dimension of my connection to the Great War, supplementing my earlier experiences as a person whose family had fought and died, and as an educator who had toured and taught on the battlefields of the Western Front. Now the War was impacting in a new way upon my understanding as a new citizen of a New World, which had believed it could escape what David Reynolds's terms the "long shadow" of the War in the century that followed.

My home state citizens are overwhelmingly both proud Americans and proud Georgians. Many times I have heard Georgians' thoughtful, honest appraisals of the state's role in the Civil War years, and candid acknowledgment of its struggles for racial equality and reconciliation, through painful eras of nineteenth century slavery and twentieth century segregation and civil rights. In short, Georgians are proud people, openly considerate of both the good and the bad in their state's past, and hopeful that Georgia's best days lie ahead for its people. Absent in much of this historic instinct in the people of Georgia is a deep understanding of the state's involvement in the Great War. Some of this is perhaps a distant echo of Georgia's initial avid opposition to entry into the War. Indeed, while many Americans sympathized with the Allied cause, Georgian traders in cotton, timber, and tobacco were vocal in their frustration with the lack of available markets due to the British naval blockade. Additionally, Wilson's mobilization of federal troops to the Mexican border included a large detachment of the Georgia National Guard, thus ensuring Georgia interest and focus on Mexico, not Germany. Widespread Georgian opposition to American intervention in the War was most singularly galvanized by the leader of the state Populist Party and Farmer's Union, Tom Watson. Before April 1917 Watson viewed Wilson's varied willingness to produce and sell arms to the Allies, publicly attack German militarism, and maintain national neutrality as a hypocritical "sham" that was inspired by Jewish and Catholic influences upon the President. In short, Georgia did not want anything to do with what it viewed as a European issue for the first years of the war.

The Zimmerman Telegram, and, sadly, national consternation about a recent lynching in Georgia, changed that position dramatically in the spring 1917, with Georgians deciding that patriotic unity was a greater priority than its own state situation. By that summer nearly 100,000 Georgian men had volunteered or been drafted, and another 250 Georgian women had joined the Nursing Corps. Georgia soon became one of the hubs for training and transportation, and new bases were established throughout the state. Even the British sent officers to Georgia's training camps. The great military reputations of contemporary U.S. regiments and units can be traced to Georgia in the First World War, with Camps Gordon and Wheeler, the latter in Macon, being the foundational home of both all-American and Dixie divisions. Additional bases at Tybee Island (Fort Screven) and at Augusta (Camp Hancock), as well as flight, engineering and transportation bases around the state, ensured that Georgia rapidly emerged as a military-strong state thereafter, with the famous infantry home of Fort Benning in Columbus breaking ground during the years of the Great War. Additionally, two of the four national internment camps for POWs were housed in Georgia, at Forts Oglethorpe and McPherson, with 800 Germans or Germany sympathizers living in the United States immediately deported to Georgia's camps within a week of the US entry. In short, Georgia's military infrastructure and "military friendly" status can trace much of its genesis to the War that Georgians bitterly opposed until it had no real choice other than participation.

This story of Georgian involvement is as personally significant to the soldiers, sailors and aviators who fought and their families as to that of any European. Not only did Georgia's politics and economics become profoundly shaped for the next century by the US participation, but the people of Georgia felt the "long shadow" too, even if their cities were not destroyed or fields turned to mud or their involvement was mercifully shorter than the other Allies. The Great War is, on the surface, a forgotten war in many ways in the United States, but only on the surface. While most people are unsure of the details and history of the War, only a little exploration uncovers many personal connections. Indeed, my interest and local publicizing of the Coleman Hill Memorial quickly prompted a wave of stories of family connections and reflections that resonate in Georgian lives. Two brief examples illustrate this.

Creek My friend Joan Godsey is a well-known and much-admired Maconite. She was for twenty-seven years the First Lady of Mercer University, married to the former President and now University Chancellor, Rev. Dr. R. Kirby Godsey. She is an accomplished musician, benefactor, and philanthropist, and a women's lay leader at one of Macon's most historic churches, First Baptist of Christ. I have known Joan for three years, but only after sharing my Coleman Hill story did she inform me of family history from the War that is central to her life, her history and that of her family. Private I. L. Stockstill, of Company F of the 4th US Infantry was a veteran of the War and the subsequent occupation of Germany, and he was Joan's father. Notably, his experiences were meticulously recorded and published in the *Picayune Item* newspaper in Picayune, Mississippi, in 1919. For Pvt. Stockstill sent back a journal to the newspaper over an unknown period. His journal and travelogue were clearly intended to be read by the public, covering a period from the closing stages of the hostilities through his return the following summer of 1919. The accounts were published in full and Joan is fortunate to hold several copies of the original Picayune newspaper. Like many veterans, Pvt. Stockstill observed much of ordinary life, detailed the towns and people he visited. He recorded for his readers back home in Mississippi the nature of the journey to Liverpool, England and then onto France and Germany, and provided personal context to the picture of a devastated Europe and being part of an Army of Occupation while the Great Powers began the slow road to the Treaty of Paris and the false hopes of the future.

Private Stockstill charts his journey from New York City to the convoy ships in Montreal, Canada, setting sail on the British ship *Demasthenes* on 8 October 1918 bound for Liverpool. His account was factual, not emotional, about the presence of a threatening U-Boat during the ten day journey, but does admit to some relief when the British naval support convoy arrives to chase off the submarine. Joan's father may have heard the British Tommy pick-me-up song "Pack up your troubles in your old kit bag, and smile, smile, smile"[2] as he camped in rainy Northern France, though for him his hatred of the phrase "roll up" to denote the rolling and unrolling of his kit bag in wet, squalid conditions is what bothers him. Like his Tommy comrades, Pte. Stockstill would have been issued the standard Brodie helmet, oddly resembling an inverted plate, but actually well designed to prevent shrapnel falling on neck and shoulders. But the dramatic irony of his account is the coincidence and timing by which Pvt. I.L. Stockstill arrives at the front line trenches literally as the Armistice is about to come into effect. In his words to the readers of the *Picayune Item*:

> On the 8th (November) we again took box cars to the front. We were there (in the Toul Sector) when the firing ceased on Nov. 11th. I tell you there was some firing going on between 10 and 11 o'clock but after 11 it seemed very much like a storm had passed. I was at the time serving in the reserve (trench) but the following day would have found me in the front lines, so you see what a few hours meant.[3]

While we might imagine Stockstill's immense relief at missing front line duty by eight hours, and the fortunes of birth, life, and family thus assured for Joan Godsey and his other offspring, the very next line of his journal reveals that Pvt. Stockstill did not view his life's

---

[2] The lyrics are from a World War I marching song written in 1915 in London by Welsh songwriters and brothers George Henry Powell and Felix Powell.

[3] *Picayune Item*, June 15, 1919.

worth at that time in what he could bequeath through genealogy, but rather in his missing the opportunity to fulfil his soldiering duty:

> Deprived of a privilege that I shall no doubt never enjoy we soon after took train back to Ligny…once more doing "squads right and left."[4]

Private Stockstill remained part of the Army of Occupation, recounted in his newspaper journal the German retreat after the Armistice back across the Rhine, and the awkwardness of him and his American comrades marching literally hours behind them. He provided extensive illustration of conditions in Germany at a time of post-war trauma and political upheaval, following the fall of the Kaiser. His family records also include a postcard dated June 1919 from an unknown comrade called Jim, noting the words "we want to go home," and an election leaflet in which Pvt. Stockstill seeks election in Picayune to the role of Sheriff and Tax Collector. The leaflet asks for the public's vote though recognizes his absence in the Army of Occupation "on account of a duty to perform (that means) he has not been permitted to see the voters in person." Joan Godsey is fortunate to have the records of her father's service in France and Germany in and after the Great War. Her family history was absolutely bound in the experience and survival of a man who, like millions of others, found themselves in

---

[4] *Picayune Item*, June 15, 1919.

the midst of a historic watershed. What Joan's long and kindly and good life has shown is that we build our world on some sure footings, but also on some random chances. In the six hours between the 5:00 A.M. signing of the Armistice and its coming into effect six hours later at 11:00 A.M., those 3,000 Allies who died on the Western Front included hundreds of Americans seeking to capture the opposite bank of the Aisne River in the Meuse-Argonne Offensive. That chance difference of eight hours in Pvt. Stockstill's life on that fateful day would have profound family ramifications—a century later we know how valuable—that he could not envision.

The re-dedication and use of the Coleman Hill Memorial prompted another equally important but less detailed story. At the time of the first recommemoration ceremony at the Memorial on 11 November 2014, led by citizens from the city and staff from my University, an elderly veteran in full Air Force uniform stood to attention throughout the event. Afterwards I received a letter from him and an invitation to meet. Joseph N. Neel III was an airman who had fought in the Korean War, and had continued his career in the clothing business after leaving service. He had returned to Macon after the Korean War, and was an active citizen and a member of the Macon Rotary. The rededication of the Memorial had moved and inspired Mr. Neel to share his story with me over several exchanges and conversations. He was the proud son of a decorated American air pilot of the Great War. His father was one of a few pioneers who led the new form of aerial warfare and was part of the Air Service of the American Expeditionary Force that was the predecessor to today's United States Air Force, established in 1947. In early 1918 his father had flown as part of the 1st Pursuit Group (a collective of squadrons) out of Toul, France in Nieuport twenty-eight aircraft that initially did not have fitted machine guns. Joe Neel Sr. was part of an American air war effort that produced more than 1,400 sorties and was responsible for the destruction of fifty enemy balloons and 151 aircraft. Other groups followed the 1st Pursuit Group that final summer of the War, flying over combat terrain, producing by Armistice Day the destruction of 781 enemy planes and seventy-three balloons. The price was high, however, with over 237 American aviators killed or MIA by the War's end.

Joe Neel had memorabilia from the War and the 1920s that highlighted his father's career. The medals, fading photographs, and other documentation he showed me were maintained with care and pride, and there were newspaper cuttings from earlier decades in which his father's career in the Great War had gained local publicity. But Joe Neel confided that he rarely had an opportunity to highlight his father's service and that there was little interest or memory of the War among most Americans, its role eclipsed by later American participation in World War Two, Korea, Vietnam, and beyond. For him, the public attention on the Memorial was a deeply personal and appreciated change in the public's focus on the Great War and an opportunity for individuals to consider how their lives had been shaped by a forgotten War in which many Americans had served and died. Mr. Neel wrote a letter of thanks to Middle Georgia State University, and expressed his hope that as the centennial of American participation came closer the University would highlight the role of the Great War, and how embedded its course and consequences are in local lives and families in Georgia and the US. His life's work understood the importance of the past and how it impacted the present, not only in his and his father's air military service, but in his leadership of Macon's oldest downtown business, the Jos. N. Neel menswear store which his grandfather had opened in 1886. Mr. Joe N. Neel III passed away a few months after our encounter and conversations, in May of 2015. His century old story had been told anew to a new generation and a new audience before he passed, and its message would continue to project forward beyond his life.

Mr. Neel's wish for greater commemoration in Georgia and the United States appears to be getting some satisfaction. Mirrored at the state level, and as a subsidiary of the National World War I Centennial Commission that Congress created in 2013, Governor Nathan Deal and the Georgia General Assembly in May 2015 established the Georgia World War I Centennial Commission, with the task "to honor, educate and commemorate." I serve on the Advisory Board to the voluntary Georgia Commission, which is comprised of academics, veterans and citizens who are leading the effort to ensure Georgia fulfills that tri-part mission of honoring, educating, and commemorating. The efforts of the Commission, as the state and nation lives through the American centennial years, is focused on highlighting historic sites and memorials, holding centennial events and educational sessions, and publicizing efforts to raise public interest and awareness. There is also an expanded Memorial Book, digitized from a database, which builds on the original 1921 Georgia State Memorial Book. A Foundation raises private, business and philanthropic funds for the work of the Commission, with no appropriated funds from state or federal sources. Clearly the national and state commissions present the most compelling opportunity for the Great War's story to resonate with renewed interest, and the centennial years present Americans with profound resources and reason to understand how our lives, collectively and individually, were shaped a century ago in ways we often fail to see.

The case for understanding is a powerful one. However compelling neutrality had been prior to engagement, the anguished understanding of engagement that President Woodrow Wilson finally came to terms with redefined an American consciousness that changed its identity and international relations for one hundred years, until perhaps the presidencies of Barack Obama and Donald Trump. For Wilson's appeal to Congress, and through Congress to the American people, was for America to enter the conflict in order to "make the world safe for democracy." This concept of America being the protector of democracy, the police force of the world, and the beacon to others, has prevailed over the past century, at a high cost of life and resources, but with noble intention for the most part. Only in recent years has American willingness to withdraw from that primary role changed the Wilsonian challenge.

In this sense President Wilson's appeal to the nation at the American entry into the War was more successful that his appeal to the international community at its conclusion. Wilson's famous "Fourteen Points" Program which he issued ten months prior to the Armistice envisioned a world of self-determination, a League of Nations for conflict resolution, and an economic model of free markets. His idealism had no place though in the psychology of the British and French at Versailles, who were determined to punish Germany and exclude her from future voice in world affairs. And Wilson's failure to bring Congress along with his plan, cemented by his unwillingness to take any Republicans to the Paris peace process, ensured that his policy of détente and inclusivity was torn to shreds in the June signing of the Treaty of Paris. While Pvt. Stockstill was waiting to end his service in the Army of Occupation in the 1919, Wilson was a few miles away facing the humiliation of watching his idealistic plan ripped apart by the vindictive, authoritarian instincts of his Allies. History denotes the Treaty as a disaster for Wilson, who returned to a country that would reject his League of Nations plan and his leadership. But history allows us to view events through our prisms, and given the pre-War imperialism that had brought disaster to the world, and the post-War fascism that would soon bring it again to even more destruction, Wilson's solutions appear more noble than those his detractors ever provided.

Private Stockstill returned home in late 1919 with his victorious comrades, and his life continued as a private citizen, but forever changed. In two short years the United States had mobilized four million personnel, and sent one million to France, at a rate of 10,000 a day by the time of the Armistice. One-hundred and twenty-thousand American servicemen died in combat over a fifteen month period, about twice as many Americans who paid the ultimate price in the entire Vietnam War. Another third of a million Americans were physical and psychological casualties of the Great War, and another 40,000 troops soon died to the Spanish Influenza that ravaged the world. Private Stockstill's journal records one of his comrades in his sleeping quarters dying of influenza on the convoy ship home. The seventy-nine names on the Coleman Hill memorial belong to an imaginary list that is 10 million names long, of all the dead combatants of the Great War. The names of another 25 million who were surviving casualties but with new pains, such as my grandfather Horace, are only known individually to families, and some to regimental and service record documents. By the 11th hour of the 11th day of the 11th month, France had lost forty percent of all its men aged between twenty and thirty-two years of age in four short years. What this cataclysm meant for humanity has been amply studied. What it meant for the individual persons and their future families is the stuff of what makes us who we are and how we give identity and meaning to our experiences. The Great War is indeed personal to us, and its personal connections give us clue not only to what we have received, but also to what we may pass onto our future generations.

10.

Daddy, What Did You Do in the Great War?

This account has been a genealogy and not a history, but it does seek to derive its content by interpreting and reinterpreting key historical events, in this case largely from some of my specific family members. The title of this final chapter, derived from an artifact (a famous 1914 British poster) of the Great War, shows us well that people repeatedly construct core understandings of themselves and their past within the context of core family relations, in a manner that includes but goes beyond the usual criteria and standards of what we commonly mean by "history." Family history instead takes its form and its function both as history and as story.

That poster, featuring a seated father and two children, was a masterful piece of propaganda. The children ask their father what he did in the Great War. His silence represents the guilt and shame of all who have no answer. The children of any honorable father—such as a daughter reading a War book on her father's lap and a son playing toy soldiers at his feet—would surely expect nothing less of their Daddy, so the propaganda message conveyed. This motif of honor and pride, reminiscent of

A WAR OF PROPAGANDA

First World War recruiting poster, playing on the guilt of those who did not volunteer 1915. Part of the British Government's attempts to stimulate support for Lord Kitchener's volunteer army.

Savile Lumley (d. 1950) UK, 1915, lithograph. © Imperial War Museum

Wilfred Owen's poetic "Ram of Pride" cited at the start of this book, would inspire every good father, husband, and son to leave family loved ones to do their duty for King and Country, so the propagandist surmised.

The historical poster also reminds us that we do indeed interpret the past from within our lives and those closest to us. In short, subjectivity has its place in the process of understanding the past, especially our own. Kierkegaard's claim that "subjectivity is truth" may cause alarm to empiricists and rationalists, but one of his other claims perhaps speaks more powerfully to the role of genealogy in making sense of the personal past, namely that "Life can only be understood backward; but it can only be lived forward."

My interest in a family genealogy of the Great War is likely influenced even by the specific historic circumstances and era of my own childhood. As a child of the 1960s I was being raised by parents and grandparents in a decade that David Reynolds[1] has powerfully detailed as a huge turning point in the British retrospective and understanding of the Great War. Drawing upon 1920s sociological insights, he argues that there is a powerful relationship between "communicative" remembrance (direct handed-on stories) and "collective" or cultural memory. By 1960, the date of my birth, the Great War for the British was being remembered radically different-

[1] David Reynolds, *The Long Shadow: The Legacies of the Great War in the Twentieth Century* (New York: W.W. Norton, 2013).

ly than in 1920, driven by the realities of unfolding decades that had experienced a far more costly Second World War, and also by the imminent passing of the Great War generation, with hundreds of thousands of its veterans dying annually. In short, according to Reynolds, a new way of seeing the past was gaining momentum just at the point when I would have been hearing my family members recount their individual memories of the 1914–18 war, and begin to communicate the cultural, collective memory of its significance. Reynolds draws attention to the power of literature, television (especially the ground-breaking 1964 BBC documentary The Great War, which was watched with record viewings), theatre, and poetry, all of which launched a retrospective re-interpretation of the War. For Reynolds, this poses problems for the historian of the War. But for the narrator, story-teller and poet, I suggest this is how we make much sense of our dialogue, the two-way street, that is our understanding and relationship with the past, and which Kierkegaard suggests is critical to our own living forward.

Genealogy then gives us a permission that pure history does not. It invites us to reflect, consider, comment, create, and imagine, more freely than the historian. This is not to suggest that it is better or worse, but rather it is different, with a different purpose. It also means that as we live our lives forward, our dialog with the past will incorporate additional layers of interpretation on the basis of new personal experiences, as well as the ever-changing narratives of our collective, cultural consciousness. How Britain viewed the Great War in 1964, at the 50th anniversary of its outbreak, is not how Britain viewed it in 2014, at the centennial. How my father understood it at the 50th anniversary is not how I understand it now, nor likely how I might interpret it in another twenty-five years. The interest in genealogy has, in fact, taken on heightened public fascination in recent years. While literature and history have always sought to connect us individually and culturally with our past, we now have the scientific—and commercially accessible—tools to trace our individual identities through chemical analysis of DNA to the places and spaces that once we could only conjecture. A vast industry of genealogical research now exists in our collective imagination and economic markets, to enable us to scientifically discover and then project our individualism onto a cosmic screen of the evolution of humankind. Our yearning for our past, and our specific human locus, has rushed to embrace this narrative of scientism in recent years through a modern western mythology of Amazon commercialism, but it reveals the same need and desire that in eastern cultures has been celebrated for millennia. The spiritual nature of that search for our connection to our specific past is well celebrated in the Shinto faith, often wrongly misrepresented in the west as "ancestor worship." Instead, Shintoism actually seeks to affirm the dialog of present and past, to establish a future life of goodness, harnessing the love and the lives of those who made us and are still therefore part of our present. Christianity has taught a similar connectedness across time and space, across life and death, within a broader family than a biological one in its doctrine of "the communion of saints," expressed in the Nicene Creed that is prayed each Sunday.

This commitment to a deeper sense of self in the context of past family has underpinned my search for my family's story of the Great War. So what then are the telling messages about my family that I believe the Great War left in the lives of those with whom I share the same DNA and have shaped me through the decades? To that question I address my final thoughts.

Firstly, despite the pointless loss, agony and sacrifice that pervasively re-shaped the collective narrative of the War from the middle of the 20th century, I never experienced in my genealogy that same pessimism or sense of waste. Indeed, the reality of my grandfathers was one of lives lived forward with hope, progress and commitment to a future, founded on a quiet respect for past events, however tortuous, that had shaped them. Whatever the trauma and loss of the War years, it did not apparently rob them of their hearts or their souls. They were able to come to terms with grief and trauma, and "pack up their troubles in their old kit bag."

It was perhaps for the great poets of the War, interestingly less than half of whom actually served on the Front, to communicate a desperation and anger that informed later generations. Ironically, the War poets perhaps knew that their voices were not necessarily speaking on behalf of a forgotten generation of Tommies, but rather to a new generation of Tommies' children. In his poem, *The General*, Siegfried Sassoon gives expression to a subtle but important discrepancy between the attitude of the poet who draws attention to the horrific effects of the War, and that of Tommy Atkins or Gunner Lewis Blake or Infantryman Horace Wood who have to act upon their duties. Sassoon, the soldier officer also seeking to be the prophetic voice, speaks in first person voice in *The General*: "we're cursing his staff for incompetent swine." But not the ordinary Tommy, who in the same poem finds the General a benign and heartening symbol: "He's (the General) a cheery old card', grunted Harry to Jack, As they slogged up to Arras with rifle and pack." This is not to suggest that the war poets were somehow wrong or exaggerated, but that their evocations were supplemented by new life-giving experiences in most of the veterans who returned to re-build their lives after the War years of destruction. I can hear in my mind Lewis Blake describing his General as a "cheery old card," and laughing out loud in good humor, "Fall In," with a smile on his face. These minutiae moments, the interstices of life, carry the light that gives clue to and shines upon the souls of people. It is clear to me that the wounded healers are those who may be burdened by pain but do not transmit it. It is equally clear that the pain of the War was not in any enduring way transmitted by my grandfathers. Today, in the litanies of personality psychology from William James to Angela Duckworth, grit or resilience is celebrated as an essential quality of personality for a successful or *highly effective life*. By that measure, my grandfathers possessed more grit than most of us could dig in a long day from a quarry.

One enduring illustration of this genealogical capacity for endurance and paradox within the War generation is found in two famous figures of central importance to the course of the War. Earlier it was noted that Field Marshall Sir John French, also titled the First Earl of Ypres, was the supreme Commander-in-Chief of the British Expeditionary Force until his replacement by Lord Douglas Haig in late 1915. A more senior role in the prosecution of the War could not be assigned. Yet during his tenure and through to the Armistice his connection and love for his sister, Charlotte Despard, remained undiminished. The extraordinary nature of this bond is not its genealogical proximity, but the context in which it thrived. For Charlotte Despard was a leading figure of the anti-war movement, a notable Suffragette, and a campaigner in the east end of London for the rights of Irish nationalism and the Sinn Fein movement for independence, which lay behind the Easter Uprising of 1916. Not only were French's and Despard's passions and energies diametrically opposed, but more powerful still was the fact that they routinely visited each other's environments, she taking trips to see her brother on the Western Front, and he sitting in church and labor union halls in London listening to Suffragette demands for the vote and the end to the War. The resilience of their relationship was a hallmark of a generation that found the capacity to endure a crisis of culture as well as that of individual conscience.

I also suggest that this resilience was not simply an act of courage or solitary agency on their part, but a core element of a structure that is the cultural myth of the English lion-heart and the Churchillian bulldog, animal symbols of power in Britain's history and story. Literary equivalents still prevail in the vernacular, such as "mustn't grumble" and "keep calm and carry on," the latter newly re-popularized in witty ways after its genesis originally as a British government message to the people during the desperate and lonely days of the London Blitz and Britain's solitary struggle against an ascendant Nazi Germany. That sense of endurance is common to the War effort and post-war lives of its combatants. For my family, that quality allowed my veteran grandfathers to build long post-war lives of productivity, changed after the Armistice into the service of the common good rather than the destruction of an enemy. For the nation, and its experience of two world wars, the acceptance of pain and fortune, suffering and success, tears and laughter was deeply ingrained into a national psyche by the time of my birth. Rudyard Kipling's line from his poem *If*, "if you can face triumph and disaster and treat those two impostors just the same," has in a way enshrined a certain temperament that sustained national and individual growth through times of fortune and misfortune, of which both World Wars epitomized the most powerful and significant example. This is not peculiar in any sense to the twentieth century and its nation states. The endurance of Judaism over millennia, and its histories and genealogies of exile and return, speaks to the capacity and power of cultural memory to ensure an enduring collective future. That cultural hope was evident in my grandfathers. I have no knowledge of how some individuals are able to make a journey from darkness to light, such as Private Stockstill who returned from France and Germany to seek public service as an elected official, while others are less able to do so. To this day I am grateful that my grandparents were similarly able to make that journey, since it gave my life and that of my parents the inherent tendency and the example of family history toward valuing life, love and hope.

This genealogy illustrates another individual and collective experience, that of the dialectic of order and disorder. The entropic state of disorder appears not only to have foundations in universal mathematics and physics, but can be measured in catastrophic human terms in the Great War. From the moment when the fragile equilibrium of a balance of competing powers in consequential relationships was upended with the Archduke's assassination at Sarajevo, the order of the times was thrown into an era of chaos and randomness, intentionality and unpredictability, co-joined to deadly effect. I have in my possession a small manual, titled Trench Orders for the Army 4th Division. The choice of words for a product with such a purpose could not be more painfully ironic. The notion that order could be produced in the trenches of the war seems pathetically desperate, yet the stories that abound show that routine, regulated behavior and repetitions of daily actions were all highly prized by both enlisted men and their officers. The attempt to orchestrate order and predictability in place of randomness and disorder seems to lie at the heart of human endeavor and aspiration. The duties and regulations listed in Trench Orders are exhausting and reassuring, though from historical hindsight possible to view with incredulity and pathos. For example, troops are instructed that "notice boards will be placed in each section's trench, on which will be pinned, daily, all orders regarding working parties," and, "before dusk, while there is still sufficient light, each gun will be laid on some particular spot either in or behind the enemy's front line." For Gunner Lewis Blake in the artillery he would have been expected "at all times (to attend) to horse management and care of equipment and management, harness and saddlery," and when running communications lines, ensure they were "laid as low as possible, preferably not more than about nine inches from the floor of the trench secured to the side of the trench by means of wire staples."

This attention to routine and order became embedded in my grandfathers' lives as they appeared to me across the generations. In a decade of upheaval, my earliest 1960s memories are of a grandparent generation that cherished order and peace. Their attention to stability, their care for their physical and domestic environment, and their commitment to daily routines was a facet I recall vividly from childhood memory of my grandfather Lewis and then of family stories about Horace. While these traits of behavior cannot be located to any one source, it is clear their War experiences absolutely reinforced such an outlook. Tommy Atkins' experiences would have craved certainty and structure, even during the interminable dullness and quiet of trench life between explosions of chaotic combat, when the routines of Trench Orders would be dutifully fulfilled. My Pops' garden and home decades later was a peaceful sublimation where that order could be guaranteed and its beauty enjoyed. This does not mean that the War generation returned as saints, but rather they secured the normalcy—even banality—that we know as ordinary life. During the course of researching this book I learned that my grandfather Horace was estranged from his father for many years, fortunately re-establishing their bond later in life, as a result of a family divorce. Such is the stuff of life's ordinariness that was required, and still is today, of those who knew War's extraordinariness in their youth.

This capacity of my veteran grandfathers to gain back into their lives what was most unobtainable during the War years leads me to my conclusion on the genealogical value of the Great War. Historical interest in the Great War has reached a renewed level of study again in these centennial years. The 1960s narrative of the War as pointless waste and the 1990s narrative of its great remembrance of national sacrifice are each under scrutiny as new interpretations are offered in these centennial years. I shall leave it to the professional historians to offer their contemporary interpretations of the Great War, but it does appear that history is indeed in the process of revising its judgment again. At the British centennial of the outbreak of War in 2014, Niall Ferguson of Harvard University gained both academic and public attention by describing the War as "the biggest error in modern history" rather than "some great victory or dreadful crime." In short, Ferguson was articulating a view of the War that neither of the major 20th century narratives claimed. His argument, intriguingly citing Britain's decisions and role during the Napoleonic War one hundred years further removed, was that an intervention on mainland Europe was unnecessary, and that the decision to intervene as a result of the violation of Belgium was disastrous for British history and its empire, robbing Britain of choice over its actions and their timing (*The Guardian*, 29 January, 2014). Ferguson points out facts rarely mentioned, such as that it cost Britain three times as much to kill a Central Powers soldier as that incurred on the Central Powers in a reverse ROI analysis. The figure he quotes is that the Allies spent $36,460 in today's value on killing each enemy soldier.

This level of data analysis is new. It utilizes the capitalist idiom of cost-benefit analysis and Ferguson's thesis concludes that the Great War was too costly a price—literally—to support the contemporary honor and pride narrative that the centennial is fueling in Britain, and its Allies. His thesis appears to connect brilliantly the current tools of data analysis with traditional renditions gained over a century of perspective to arrive at a conclusion that the Great War was not so much about waste, nor about pride, but about a massive historical mistake. David Reynolds[2] suggests similar argument, that its shadow shaped the future forces that ran amok through the century. And so their arguments, which indeed could only be made in light of a century of experience, lead us to the notion that the Great War requires to be remembered and understood because it lead directly and consequentially to other great historical events and one above all else: the Second World War. This thesis becomes more compelling the more it recedes into the past. It also means that the heralded Greatest Generation of World War Two, and the Forgotten Generation of World War I, are actually one and the same family; they are just fathers and sons, of the same DNA. There is now a compelling sense in which both First and Second World Wars are one titanic event of global struggle. Wilson's "making the world safe for democracy" reinforces this view, showing that in both cataclysms the risk to the world was democracy itself, in the face of forces of militarism and totalitarianism. Ferguson may

---

[2] David Reynolds, *The Long Shadow: The Legacies of the Great War in the Twentieth Century* (New York: W. W. Norton, 2013).

be correct in the "error" thesis, but that is not my point here. What this book has sought to argue is that there are consequences lived out in the lives of the families who were engaged in the "error" or terror at the start of the 20th century. But while humankind's history may have reinforced or struggled to correct that error, family lives are given other opportunities of redemption that perhaps nations are denied. What is undeniable is that we cannot understand the forces, context, influences and decisions that we make in our lives today unless we look back at our family history. Similarly, we cannot understand the forces, context, and decisions within the human family today in its nations, organizations, and communities, unless we understand the decisions of the past, such as those made 100 years ago in the most catastrophic war of all history until that point.

The American Federal Reserve was founded one hundred years ago after a series of meetings in the years around the Great War. During those meetings the great captains of industry and owners of capital, such as Henry Hyde, William Vanderbilt and Joseph Pulitzer, would convene at the Jekyll Island Club on the coast of Georgia. On the quiet shores of Jekyll Island the financial elite, comprising one quarter of the world's wealth, determined that a new world order, being forged violently in the crucible of Europe, would need a global financial authority, that needed to be sustained and governed from the United States. They knew that the nineteenth century age of Empire, dying in the convulsions of the

Great War, would provide the platform for a new world order, financed and led by American might and American money. They realized they stood at a painful crossroads in human history, and they had the vision and the power to determine which road would hold the promise of the future for the United States.

That capacity to look back and live forward was emblematic of my veteran grandfathers, who certainly did not belong to the financial elite who were planning the twentieth century world order while the nineteenth century order died. My grandfathers did so in public ways that were gracious, successful, capable of enduring the slings and arrows of fortune, both good and bad, and only shaped, not defined, by their young years in the Great War. Their inner private lives, memories, pains, and traumas of that time were not worn on their sleeves. If there was a sense of the agony of the Great War, it was kept to the lonely spaces of the night, and not permitted to inhabit the public world of the day. Perhaps most importantly, they were capable of building families that respected the human aspiration to joy, hope, life and love. What they did is surely a lesson for all democratic persons. It is important that the Forgotten War and its generation is re-discovered here in the United States, not necessarily in the way that the Europeans have done it, but certainly in a fashion that allows Americans to learn about a past that has so powerfully shaped the nation's fortunes in the 20th century and still does today in the 21st. The post-World War II military-industrial complex; the US as a Superpower; the agonies of the Middle East; genocide in the Balkans and Africa; the Cold War and re-emerging tensions with Russia; the West's troubled relations with the Islamic world; the strained unity of the European Union; the "tiger economies" of Asia; the development of economic globalization; the fascination and threats of technology; the rise of China; and the new post-truth political discourse. These and other contemporary challenges that our Twitter feed downloads daily find their roots and branches in a war across the ocean one century ago. The War to End All Wars did nothing of the sort, but rather set a new context, a new benchmark and a new trajectory for human conflict since the 11th hour, 11th day, and 11th month Armistice delivered an illusory peace. We here in the US would be well advised not only to remember our compatriots and families that went over to that Great War in the belief of a world made safer for democracy, as charged by their president of that time, but also to recognize how their actions and struggles shaped the world that we inhabit today with the legacy that continues even at one hundred years of age.

Robert Laurence Binyon's famous poem *For the Fallen*, written in the earliest weeks of the Great War, is best known for a stanza in its middle:

They shall grow not old, as we that are left grow old:
Age shall not weary them, nor the years condemn.
At the going down of the sun and in the morning
We will remember them.[3]

Understandably, given the poem's title, we have been moved by these lines to remember with dignity and gratitude those who paid the ultimate sacrifice in the Great War. Perhaps as importantly, and with a timeliness that a centennial offers us, we now need to attend as carefully to the second sentence. Our lives, with the rising and setting of the sun each day, have been the creation of our family generations of the past, just as we today are nurturing the family generations of tomorrow. We remember not only because it is proper to honor those lying in Flanders fields and all the resting places of the Great War's fallen, but we remember also because that titanic era is still shaping what we think, how we act, and what we see, each and every day that the sun rises and the sun sets.

[3] Robert Laurence Binyon, "For the Fallen," in the *Times* of London, 21 September 1914.

BIBLIOGRAPHY

Barker, Pat. *Regeneration*. London: Viking Press, 1991.

Barker, Pat. *The Eye in the Door*. London: Viking Press, 1993.

Barker, Pat. *The Ghost Road*. London: Viking Press, 1995.

Davis, Richard Harding, *New York Tribune*, 23 August 1914.

Doyle, Peter & Chris Foster. *What Tommy Took to War 1914-1918*. Shire: Oxford University Press, 2014.

Ferguson, Niall. "Britain Entering First World War was Biggest Error in Modern History." *The Guardian*, 29 January 2014.

H.B.M. Government. *Trench Orders 4th Division*. Replica by Memorabilia Pack, Edinburgh, 1914.

Hochschild, Adam. *To End All Wars: A Story of Loyalty and Rebellion, 1914–1918*. Boston: Houghton Mifflin Harcourt, 2011.

Larson, Erik. *Dead Wake: The Last Crossing of the Lusitania*. New York: Penguin Random House, 2015.

Lewis, Jon E., ed. *A Brief History of World War I*. London: Robinson & Running Press, 2014.

Poems of the Great War. London: Penguin Books, 1998.

Remarque, Erich Maria. *All Quiet on the Western Front*. New York: Little, Brown & Co., 1929.

Reynolds, David. *The Long Shadow: The Legacies of the Great War in the Twentieth Century*. New York: W.W. Norton, 2013.

Sassoon, Siegfried, *The Old Huntsman and Other Poems*. New York: Holt, 1918.

Scripture Gift Mission. *The Gospel According to St. John*. London, 1914.

Sheffield, Gary. *The First World War in 100 Objects*. London Andre Deutsch Ltd., 2013.

RECOMMENDED READING:

BBC Three. *Our World War* (TV Series): Netflix, 2014.

Berg, Scott A., ed. *World War I and America: Told by the Americans Who Lived It.* New York: Library of America, 2017.

Doyle, Peter. *The British Soldier of the First World War.* Oxford: Shire Publications, 2011.

Follett, Ken. *Fall of Giants.* New York: Dutton, 2010.

Gerwarth, Robert. *The Vanquished: Why the First World War Failed to End.* New York: Farrar, Straus & Giroux, 2016.

Hart, Peter. *The Great War: A Combat History of the First Word War.* Oxford: Oxford University Press, 2013.

Hill, Duncan. *The Great War: A Pictorial History.* Hertfordshire: Atlantic, 2013.

Keegan, John. *The First World War.* New York: Vintage Books, 2000.

Mayo, Virginia, ed. *Harry's War: A British Tommy's Experience in the Trenches in World War One.* London: Conway, 2008.

Meyer, G. J. *The World Remade: America in World War I.* New York: Bantam Books, 2016.

Neiberg, Michael S., *The Path to War: How the First World War Created Modern America.* New York: Oxford University Press, 2016.

Neidell, Indy. The Great War-www.thegreatwar.tv, YouTube-Channell, 2014.

Rubin, Richard. *The Last of the Doughboys: The Forgotten Generation and Their Forgotten World War.* New York: Mariner, 2014.

Solzhenitsyn, Alexander. *August 1914.* London: Book Club Associates, 1972.

Willmott, H.P. *World War I.* London: Dorling Kindersley Ltd., 2009.

Index

INDEX